PENGUIN BOOKS

Nor and Zen

Roy..Stowe ... is chief priest of the Rinzai temple Ryutanji
and the author of numerous books on Zen.

Now and Zen

Notes from a
Buddhist Monastery

with Illustrations

Eiyū Murakoshi

Translated by
Meredith McKinney

PENGUIN BOOKS

PENGUIN BOOKS

UK | USA | Canada | Ireland | Australia
India | New Zealand | South Africa

Penguin Books is part of the Penguin Random House group of companies
whose addresses can be found at global.penguinrandomhouse.com.

First published in Japan as *Irasuto de yomu Zen no hon*
by Suzuki shuppan 1998
This translation published in Penguin Books 2020

002

Set in 9.2/12.5 pt ITC Century Std
Typeset by Jouve (UK), Milton Keynes
Printed and bound in Great Britain by Clays Ltd, Elcograf S.p.A.

A CIP catalogue record for this book is available from the British Library

ISBN: 978–0–241–43375–1

www.greenpenguin.co.uk

MIX
Paper from
responsible sources
FSC® C018179

Penguin Random House is committed to a
sustainable future for our business, our readers
and our planet. This book is made from Forest
Stewardship Council® certified paper.

Contents

Contents

Preface

In Japan we have an expression, 'Float like cloud, flow like water'. It means to live free and unconstrained, like a floating cloud or flowing water. The Japanese word *unsui*, literally 'cloud and water', comes from this expression. The word originally referred to a monk who freely wanders the land in search of spiritual teachers. '*Unsui*' is now used specifically to refer to a monk of the Zen sect, but it's rare for *unsui* these days to wander the land searching for teachers. Nowadays a monk usually spends years in one place of training or *dōjō*, practising under a single teacher.

I too spent many years in a *dōjō* of the Rinzai school of Zen Buddhism. My teacher was the late *rōshi* (Zen teacher) Suzuki Sochū, but Nakagawa Sōun, who was Suzuki's teacher, was still alive then, and I had the good fortune to indirectly receive his teachings too. I was lucky to be able to do this simultaneously at the same *dōjō* – usually monks have to move to a different place to receive the teachings of another Zen teacher.

These two teachers were complete opposites.

There was no mistaking the strictness of the man who was my direct teacher, Sōchū Rōshi. The mere sight of him was enough to tell you. Sōun Rōshi, on the other hand, emanated the tenderness of a grandfather fondly watching over his grandchildren. Nevertheless, Sōchū taught me gently and carefully the correct meditation posture and method of breathing, while old Sōun would simply come out with mild remarks like, 'Oh, just spend some time looking at the plum blossoms,' a casual suggestion tossed your way which in fact hid an incredibly deep and rigorous teaching.

What they both had in common was kindness in their teaching of what is termed 'the Law' (hō), the Buddhist doctrine. Needless to say, this didn't apply only to myself – they were equally benign to all the novice monks who had gathered there under their guidance.

This book about the Zen teachings and monastic life is based on my experience of the teachings of these two rōshi.

Of course, I myself am still lacking in my practice, so I'm far from confident that I can properly convey the truth about Zen. But my plan is to try to make this book enjoyable to read and easy to understand, weaving in illustrations as I go along. Please keep me company on the journey, and perhaps when you finish reading you might find yourself thinking, 'Why don't I go along to a bookshop and find something that will teach me a bit more about Zen?', or perhaps, 'Why don't I try joining a zazen meditation group?' It would make me happy to think that this book might be the means by which you come in contact with the Buddhist teachings.

Eiyū Murakoshi

1

What is the Collection of
Secret *Kōans*?

How *Kōans* Work

The Relationship between Kōans
and Maths Questions

When I came to write this book I spent some time wondering how best
to begin, and I decided to start with the *kōan*, the meditation method
that typifies the Rinzai school of Zen that I belong to.

So just what is a *kōan*?

Here's the dictionary definition:

> A question given to the Zen practitioner for contemplation, as a
> means to his or her enlightenment. *Kōans* are derived from the
> words and deeds of eminent practitioners, and lead one to a realm
> that transcends the world of everyday thought.

So *kōans* are a kind of manual to lead the Zen practitioner to enlightenment.

The practitioner in the *dōjō*, or place of practice, is given a *kōan*
by the teacher and ponders it while sitting *zazen*, bringing an answer
to the teacher in a one-on-one interview several times a day. The con-
versation between teacher and student during this interview is known
in Zen as a *mondō*, or 'question-and-answer'. There's a common belief
that a *mondō* is some special and incomprehensible exchange that
transcends ordinary understanding, but this isn't so.

A *kōan* is . . . well, you could say it's a bit like a maths problem.

This kind of statement runs the risk of getting me into hot water with my superiors – but please don't be angry! It's just that comparing *kōans* to maths problems seems to provide an easy way to explain their mechanism.

As to just how the two are similar, well for a start a maths problem has a Question part and an Answer part, right? A *kōan* is also made up of a Question part and an Answer part.

Think back to when you were in your early years at school. Remember those maths exercises you had to do for homework? You were only given the Questions part – the Answers page was removed, because of course if it was there kids would just copy the answer without working it out for themselves. Then back at school next day there would be an Answers session in class.

There is also an Answers session in the *dōjō*. It's known as *sanzen*.

A special small room, called a *sanzen* room, is set aside in the *dōjō* for the *sanzen*. Here the Zen teacher sits, quietly waiting for the practitioners to come.

From outside in the nearby corridor comes the slow striking of a little gong, rung by the monk who's been assigned this task. This is the sign that the *sanzen* period has begun.

When this gong is rung, the monks who have been meditating in the meditation hall come running out. Then, with a single stroke of the gong, a practitioner enters the *sanzen* room. When each *mondō* interview is finished, the teacher rings a little bell. On hearing this, the next practitioner strikes the gong then enters the *sanzen* room.

As for why there's this unseemly dash to *sanzen* in a place that's supposed to be strictly silent, this is apparently a hangover from the old days when there were great numbers of monks – unlike today – and it was simply a question of first come, first served.

These *sanzen* sessions occur either three times a day, morning noon and evening, or twice a day, morning and evening.

There is also sometimes a more formal event called a *sōsan*, in which all the monks must meet the teacher one by one in order of rank.

2

OK, let's get back to the comparison between *kōans* and maths exercises.

Another way in which the two are similar is that in both there's only one answer. Just as the exercise '1+1= ?' has the answer '2', there is a given answer equivalent to that '2' for each *kōan*.

Imagine, for example, that a certain *kōan* has the answer 'forest'. That is precisely what the answer must be. A similar answer such as 'trees' or 'woodland' would be incorrect. There is only one answer.

Also, just as the level of difficulty gets higher as you go through the pages of a maths book, the stages in Zen advance as you go further in *kōan* study. But please don't get me wrong – there's no guarantee that at a certain stage you will arrive at enlightenment.

OK, let's take an example from a work called *Mumonkan*, or *The Gateless Barrier*. This is a collection of forty-eight *kōans* written in Sung dynasty China by a monk called Mumon Ekai. Here's the first one, called 'Chao-chou's Dog'. It's actually written in Chinese, which might seem odd if you think of Zen as Japanese, but you have to remember that many Zen texts were originally written in China (where Zen is called Ch'an), and this *kōan* collection is one of them.

There's a bit that comes before, but the actual *kōan* part says:

A monk asked Master Chao-chou, 'Does a dog have a buddha nature or not?'
    Chao-chou answered 'not' (*Mu*).

'What?' you'll probably say. 'Surely the answer's already given in the *kōan*! The dog doesn't have a buddha nature.' And yes, you might think that the monk's words are the *kōan* question and the master's words are its answer, like this:

QUESTION: A monk asked Master Chao-chou, 'Does a dog have a buddha nature or not?'
ANSWER: Chao-chou answered 'not' (*mu*).

And in that case you'd be right, of course – the answer is that a dog doesn't have buddha nature.

But unfortunately it doesn't work like that. This whole passage is actually the Question, the equivalent of the '1 + 1 = ?' part of a maths question.

Every book about *kōans* says that they are Zen questions, but the problem is that word 'question' – here we have an example that includes an answer. Please take good note of this, because it's important at this stage for an understanding of the nature of *kōans*.

If you sit before the teacher and say, 'The answer to the *kōan* about whether a dog has the Buddha nature or not is what Chao-chou said – not (*mu*),' the teacher will say, 'Go away and meditate on that word "*mu*".' The *sanzen* session will be over in thirty seconds flat, and you'll be out on your ear.

So now you have to find an answer equivalent to that 2 in 1 + 1 = ?.

The discussion about this answer that takes place between teacher and student is the Zen *mondō* (literally, Zen question and answer), but unfortunately it is not permitted to reveal the answers to *kōans*, so I can't tell you what that 2 is!

The Similarities Between *Kōans* and Maths Problems

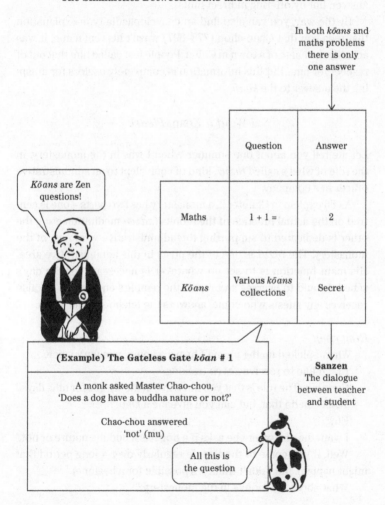

In both *kōans* and maths problems there is only one answer

	Question	Answer
Maths	$1 + 1 =$	2
Kōans	Various *kōans* collections	Secret

Kōans are Zen questions!

Sanzen
The dialogue between teacher and student

(Example) The Gateless Gate *kōan* # 1

A monk asked Master Chao-chou, 'Does a dog have a buddha nature or not?'

Chao-chou answered 'not' (mu)

All this is the question

This is why you'll seldom find much written about the answers in books that talk about *kōans*. *Kōans* aren't things to be examined and thought about rationally, they're to be meditated on.

If a dog has a buddha nature, is it a dog? Or is it a dog if not?

In this way, we explain the problem not by directly touching on the answer, but by offering indirect hints.

By the way, you can also find an encyclopaedia-type explanation that tells you that Chao-chou (778–897) wasn't his real name, it was actually the name of a town in China. People just called him that out of respect for him. But this information is completely useless for grasping the answer to the *kōan*.

I Want a Kōan, *Please*

Let me tell you about one summer when I was in the monastery, in the role of what's called *fuzui*, kind of equivalent to an administrative officer in a company.

As I'll explain in Chapter 2, a monastery has two parts – one is centred on the actual practice of the monks (*zazen* meditation etc.), the other is dedicated to supporting the administrative workings of the monastery. The *fuzui* is one of the posts in this administrative area. His main function is to set up whatever is necessary for the day's schedule, and to oversee and repair the temple's equipment. He also receives any guests who come, answers the telephone and so on.

Ring ring!

When I picked up the phone I heard a young woman's voice.

'Er, I'd like to receive *zazen* training.'

'Certainly. The rule is that you must live in the temple for nine days.'

'Yes, I can do that, but can you give me a *kōan*?'

'Eh?'

'I want the one where he asks if a dog has a buddha nature or not.'

'Well, if you come to the temple regularly over a long period that might happen, but I don't think it's possible for a beginner.'

'What about the monks in the monastery?'

6

'After they're taught the basics of how to sit *zazen* and how to breathe, the teacher will give them a *kōan*.'

'So what happened in your case?'

'Me?'

'Yes. What was the first *kōan* you were given?'

'The one about Chao-chou and the dog.'

'When did you receive it, do you remember?'

'Actually it was on the first day of December, eight months after I entered the monastery.'

'Oh dear, I can't wait that long. Couldn't I be given it on the first day if I ask nicely?'

'I don't think that's possible.'

'What if I brought along a box of bean cakes as a gift?'

'It wouldn't be possible even if you filled a cake box with bean cakes made of gold.'

'You mean gold coins?'

'That's right.'

'Oh, so you're after money, are you? Naughty!'

'No no. What I'm saying is even gold coins wouldn't work.'

'Well then, do you know of any place where I could get a *kōan* right away?'

'I'm afraid I don't.'

Beep beep beep.

The line had gone dead.

Different teachers give *kōans* in different ways, and there are also differences between the way *kōans* are used for monks and for lay practitioners. Timing and ways of presenting also differ from one person to the next. It's true that meditating on *kōans* is a characteristic of the Rinzai school of Zen, but that doesn't mean that solving *kōans* is the only aim of meditation.

In the case of maths problems, you have your answer once you've learned how to look at $1 + 1 = ?$, for instance, and come up with the solution. But with a *kōan* that's not the case – you don't find the answer just by looking at this specific question. What's more, there's no point in getting the answer if you don't then put it into practice in everyday life.

In that sense, *kōans* differ from maths problems. They work in your life. With maths, once you've got the answer you're done. With *kōans*, you take that answer and you apply it to your whole life. I know I may come across as a bit arrogant when I say this, but that's how it seems to me.

And while I'm at it, there's one more way that *kōans* are like maths questions. Remember how you had maths questions to solve for homework every day? Well, you also never take a day off from facing the teacher in those one-to-one *sanzen* sessions where you discuss your answer.

Being Stuck for an Answer Leads You to the Answer

Why Do Flags Flutter?

I hope you now have a general understanding of the structure of *kōans*. I'd like to help you learn a little more about *kōans* by taking a look at two others.

The 29th *kōan* in the *The Gateless Gate* is called 'Not the Wind; Not the Flag'. Here it is:

Hui-neng, the sixth Zen patriarch, was waiting one day to hear a Buddhist lecture. The flag that announced the lecture was fluttering nearby, and two monks began to talk about it.

Monk A: The flag is moving.

Monk B: No, the wind is moving.

Both monks insisted they were right, and they couldn't reach an agreement.

Then the sixth patriarch said to them, 'It's not the flag that's moving. It's not the wind that's moving. It's the mind that moves.'

The two monks were astonished and overawed.

In the normal way of thinking, the flag is moving because the wind is blowing. But of course, since we can't see wind, it's possible to state that it's the flag that moves. Then the sixth patriarch steps in and gives them an answer that transcends both these positions, by saying that rather than the flag or the wind, it's their own minds that are fluttering to and fro endlessly over this question.

Some readers might think, 'Right, that's pretty clever to say their minds are what is moving. These two have been distracted by this question of flag versus wind. That's very Zen.' But you would be wrong. To repeat what I emphasized in the previous section, all of this is the *question*. 'It's the mind that moves' is part of the *kōan* question, it isn't the answer to it. However if you want to know the answer, I'm sorry but I'm forbidden to reveal it. I can't say anything more.

If a practitioner sits in front of the teacher for *sanzen* and says: 'It's actually the wind that's moving.'

Or: 'It's the flag that's moving.'

Or: ' "It's the mind that is moving" is a wonderful answer', he'll be told again and again, 'No, no – go away and consider a bit more.'

Hitting this wall is a way of training the mind.

Which is the True Ch'ien?

A girl called Ch'ien was in love with a boy called Wang-chau, and he was in love with her. But her father didn't want her to marry him, so the two couldn't be together. Wang-chau was furious. He borrowed a boat and set off to try to abduct Ch'ien.

Ch'ien learned about this, and her despair was so great that she became ill.

But when Wang-chau set off in his boat, another Ch'ien appeared before him, and together they ran away.

Years later, when they had been blessed with children, Ch'ien returned to her parents' home to beg forgiveness. There she found the other Ch'ien, who had never recovered from her illness. When she approached her, the two became one.

The fifth Zen patriarch Wu-tsu (?–1104) asked a monk about this old Chinese folk tale: 'So who was the real Ch'ien: the one who ran away, or the one who lay there sick?' (*The Gateless Gate* 35, 'Which Is the Real Ch'ien?')

When her father opposed the marriage, Ch'ien's soul separated into two – Ch'ien A who loved Wu-tsu so fervently that she was prepared to run away with him, and Ch'ien B who became a mere shell of her former self from sorrow. The question is, which was the real one?

Unlike the previous two *kōans* we've looked at, this one doesn't have the *mondō* form, where a monk and a teacher talk. This is a 'direct question' *kōan*, that asks for an answer.

The teacher asks 'Which is the real Ch'ien?' It's pretty straightforward. Taken at face value, if you go to your teacher for *sanzen* and choose Ch'ien A, and that doesn't work, then next time you choose Ch'ien B: one of those has to be the right answer. You have a 50:50 chance of being right the first time, and if you aren't you're sure to be right the second time.

However . . . that's not the way it works. Remember that a *kōan* never contains its answer. A *kōan* starts its work when you're stuck for an answer, and you could say that the answer is what the practitioner and the teacher produce together.

Now let's go to the meditation hall. I'm remembering the time when my teacher Suzuki Sōchū had given me the 'Which is the real Ch'ien?' *kōan*, and I was wrestling furiously with it.

One day, as I was walking along the narrow east–west verandah of the hall, I found myself heading straight for the teacher, who was coming the other way.

I decided that the best thing to do was to go straight on without passing too close to him, but failing that I should just turn back. Irrevocably we approached each other. If this was some romantic scene of two adoring lovers moving closer and closer the heart would be beating fast with anticipation, but what I felt was more like the panic of witnessing two aircraft on a collision course.

'I'll pass him with my head lowered,' I thought – but at that moment my teacher spoke.

'Hey, do you like bean cakes?'

'Y-yes,' I stammered nervously. Beaming, the teacher took a bean cake from the sleeve of his robe, broke it in two and passed the pieces to me.

I looked at it. One of the pieces was much bigger, and the sweet bean paste inside was spilling from it.

Having handed me the broken bean cake, the teacher went on his way without a word.

That's all that happened.

Perhaps that's all that happened.

But I can't help feeling that the teacher was trying to give me a hint of some sort. Sometimes a teacher will choose an unexpected time or place to guide the practitioner. I've no idea what he had in his mind – whether that was just a bean cake, or whether it was a bean cake intended as a hint, or whether he'd simply happened to find the bean cake in his sleeve a few days after he put it there. But whatever it was, that bean cake played on my mind.

That's where I'll leave the story of the bean cake. I'll just add a little more here about *kōans*.

There are several collections of *kōans* – *The Gateless Gate (Mumonkan)*, the *Hekiganroku*, the *Rinzairoku* and others – all created in Sung dynasty China. But all the *kōans* that have come down to us in Japan today were brought together and organized by the great Japanese Zen master Hakuin (1685–1768) in his own *kōan* collection called *Types of Kōan*. In other words, our *kōans* today are based on the models made by Hakuin.

The schools of the Zen sect that use *kōans* are called *kanna zen*, which means literally 'Zen that contemplates stories'. Stories in this case means *kōans*, so this is a form of Zen in which you gain enlightenment by contemplating *kōans*.

Another form of Zen does not use *kōans* but focuses solely on meditation. The school of Zen that uses this form is Sōtō.

Different schools of Zen also have different styles of *zazen* sitting.

Contents of Types of *Kōan*

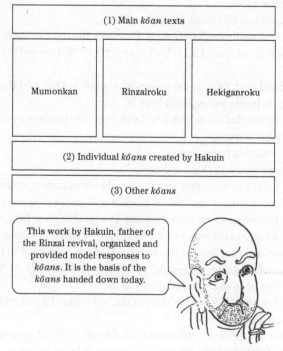

(1) Main *kōan* texts

| Mumonkan | Rinzairoku | Hekiganroku |

| (2) Individual *kōans* created by Hakuin |

| (3) Other *kōans* |

This work by Hakuin, father of the Rinzai revival, organized and provided model responses to *kōans*. It is the basis of the *kōans* handed down today.

Zen Master Hakuin

In the Sōtō style of sitting, the meditator faces the wall of the meditation hall, while in the other two Zen sects (Rinzai and Ōbaku) you face the centre of the hall.

Oh yes, and I once read somewhere that there are 1,007 *kōans* in existence, but I don't know how this number was arrived at. In the case of the first *kōan* we looked at, for example, the one about the dog, there is also a spoken version that only the teacher can give, and I don't know whether these secret *kōans* are included in the count.

Whatever the number, it's said that it takes around ten years to complete them all.

One thing is certain – both the *kōans* and their answers are shrouded in a great veil of secrecy.

How Not to be Bitten by Mosquitoes

The Greatest Enemy in the Meditation Hall

I can present the question part of *kōans* and give you a simple introduction to books about them, but as I've said above, I'm not permitted to reveal the answers. Only your teacher can talk about all this in detail, so I'm in no position to do it here.

Having said that, the story that I want to tell you now could be interpreted as a kind of hint to help you understand the nature of *kōans*. But I do want to make clear that this is a story about something that really happened, it's not an actual *kōan*.

It happened one summer, when I was meditating alongside the other monks as well as a number of people from the business world who were staying at the monastery for a while to practise meditation.

Unless the weather is particularly bad the sliding doors around the edge of the meditation hall are always left open while you sit, summer or winter.

It's hard in winter, sitting there exposed to the cold north wind whistling through. You lose all sensation in your hands and face, the bits of you that aren't protected by your robe, and it's quite common to get frostbite on your ears and fingers.

But summers are worse. As you sit there absolutely still, in almost no time you feel the sweat start to pour from you like a waterfall, from your shoulders down to your stomach, and your underwear quickly becomes wringing wet. Still, you can just resign yourself and say, 'Well it's summer after all, so it can't be helped if it's hot.'

But the real problem is the mosquitoes. All the sliding doors in the meditation hall are left wide open, so mosquitoes come thronging in.

What's more, the meditators are sitting there completely still, so they provide a perfect hunting ground for the mosquitoes. It's as though we're saying to them, 'Sure, come on over, please take as much of our blood as you want!'

And so we monks spend our summers plagued by this vast mosquito army.

Nnnnnnnnnnn!

Here comes the invasion.

They come snaking in for the attack, in close formation.

Close observation reveals that morning and evening, sunrise and sunset, are the two times of day that are really the mosquitoes' feast times.

And the mosquitoes you get in mountain temples aren't the same as the city ones. Not only the sound they make but the size of them is huge. I believe they're called Tiger Mosquitoes. They bite you on the neck, they bite you on the forehead or hands or fingers, and unfortunately in summer monks wear a light gauze robe so they have no trouble biting your crossed legs through the fabric as well.

But if you go 'Wham!' and hit one, and pick it up between finger

Just go on sitting without thought

When you're sitting you're a sitting target . . .

and thumb with a little smile of satisfaction, you can be sure this will cause you a whole new problem.

'Stop moving!' yells the senior monk, and he strides over with his long thin stick, called a *keisaku*, and whacks you three times. The ceiling of the meditation hall is high, which makes the sound echo loudly. So there's nothing for it but to wait till the time comes to swap legs in your meditation pose, and seize the moment to scratch a quick X over the latest bite before you settle down again. 'Damn you! Just you wait till the break. I'll get you well and truly then!'

I can remember how I used to sit *zazen* suppressing the desperate urge to scratch myself everywhere.

One summer afternoon, the teacher Nakagawa Sōen gave a lecture to the assembled crowd of monks and lay practitioners, using as his text the *Rinzairoku*. 'Please think about how you can avoid being bitten by mosquitoes,' he said to us. At this time he had retired from being head of the monastery and handed over to Sōchū, but he still appeared from time to time to give us guidance.

How to avoid being bitten by mosquitoes!? I thought. Well, you could come up with all sorts of solutions to that problem!

Why not use mosquito coils, for example?

Why not spray some insect repellent?

Or there are those vape mats that you can burn.

Or you could even spray the area around the temple so they can't breed.

Or wouldn't it be a great idea to get some donations together to build a new meditation hall that has air conditioning.

But realistically speaking, none of these solutions were possible. There's simply no way to avoid being bitten by mosquitoes in the meditation hall.

That mosquito army that invaded morning and evening every day continued to really get me down, and I soon forgot about the teacher's question.

Seven days later, Sōen gave another lecture.

'Did you find a way to avoid being bitten by mosquitoes?' he asked us.

Silence reigned. No doubt we were all thinking: Well, there *is* no way, is there?

Then he grinned and said, 'The way to avoid being bitten by mosquitoes is to generously make an offering to them.'

Hmmm, I said to myself. That's not much help, is it. This 'offering' is what a priest receives in thanks when they've said sutras at someone's request, such as at a funeral. I certainly didn't want to donate so much as a drop of my blood to those damned mosquitoes. I put his words out of my mind.

When You Change the Way You Think . . .

But a few days later, I began to realize that this question of the teacher's – 'How can you avoid being bitten by mosquitoes?' – was actually extremely clever.

If you think of it in terms of the way to not be bitten, you'll never come up with a solution. But that's the first step, to throw yourself into the search for an answer. After you've tried and failed again and again to provide obvious answers, you start to question the question itself. In terms of maths, you start looking at this whole '1+1=?' question.

Of course, in maths you normally don't have to get to that point. The question is the question, and you just need the answer. But in the case of solving the mosquito problem, you'll never find the solution unless you re-think the question itself.

Instead of 'How to avoid being bitten by mosquitoes' you need to re-state the question as, for example, 'How to not mind being bitten by mosquitoes'.

The key thing you have to change is that word 'avoid'. It's being stuck on that word that makes you come up with answers like 'mosquito coil' or 'insect repellent'.

Once you've gone through that process, you then look at the question from a different angle, and now you can find the solution: 'Make an offering to them'.

Let's summarize the process:

'How to Avoid being Bitten by Mosquitoes?'

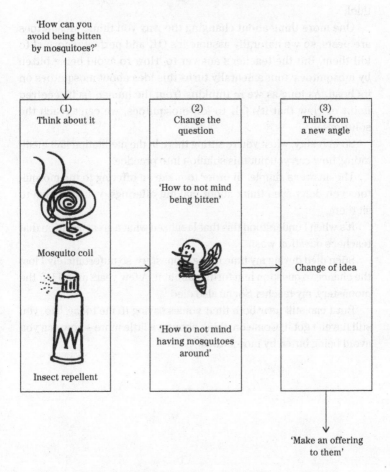

'How can you avoid being bitten by mosquitoes?'

(1) Think about it	(2) Change the question	(3) Think from a new angle
Mosquito coil	'How to not mind being bitten'	Change of idea
Insect repellent	'How to not mind having mosquitoes around'	

'Make an offering to them'

1. Trying hard to think it through in terms of the question.
2. Looking for the key word that produces your answers, and changing the way the question is expressed.
3. Using this to think from a new angle that leads you to the solution.

In other words, to solve the problem you have to change the way you think.

One more thing about changing the way you think. Mosquitoes are pests, so we naturally assume it's OK and perfectly normal to kill them. But the teacher's answer to 'How to avoid being bitten by mosquitoes' fundamentally turns this idea about mosquitoes on its head. As long as we're thinking from the human (self) centred point of view that it's OK to kill mosquitoes, we can't reach the solution.

So in reality, when you're sitting there in the meditation hall meditating, how can you put this solution into practice?

The answer's simple. In order to make an offering to the mosquitoes you don't even think about making offerings, you just have to sit there.

It's when I understood this that I realized what a great question that teacher's question was.

Sōen died during my time in the monastery, so unfortunately I lost the chance to question him further about it. A few years after I left the monastery, my teacher Sōchū also died.

But I can still hear both their voices saying to me today, 'No, you still haven't got it. Come on, think about it a little more – how can you avoid being bitten by mosquitoes?'

2

Let's Head to a Monastery

What is a Monastery Like?

Becoming a Monk

What sort of place do you think a Zen monastery is?

I spent years in one, and I'd sum it up by saying it's a different kind of heaven inside the normal everyday world. The word 'heaven' might suggest the idea of paradise to you, but of course that's not what I mean. What I'm trying to say is, it's just a completely different place from the world of everyday life.

The day starts early, meals are plain and simple, and the rule is that everyone acts as a group, which means that you hardly have any free time to yourself. The way of life in a monastery hasn't changed for hundreds of years, so really you're living in a kind of time warp. In fact, it's not the kind of place you'd choose to go unless you had a very special reason.

So what weird fate leads people to shave their heads and enter a monastery? The common ways this happens in Japan are:

1. You're the eldest son of a Zen temple family and you will inherit the position of temple priest.
2. You're drawn to enter a monastery in order to become a Zen teacher.
3. You enter as a result of some family-related matter.

I belonged to the first category, the most common one, where the eldest son of a temple family is fast-tracked to gain the qualifications to become the next generation's priest in his family temple. (The priests of local Buddhist temples serve their surrounding community. They have families, and the position of priest is hereditary.)

Those in the second group come from completely ordinary families but through reading about Zen, or attending meditation sessions, or perhaps through meeting a Zen teacher, they become passionately convinced that they must become a monk. In the third category are the men who, for instance, become a monk in order to take on the position of priest at a local Zen temple and marry the temple daughter (if there's no son to inherit the position), or who are the second son of a temple family whose older son doesn't want to inherit.

So if, as does occasionally happen, you decide you want to be a monk, how do you go about it?

In Japan, you go to a Zen temple somewhere and place yourself under the guidance of the priest there, register with his affiliated monastery, shave your head, and then you simply go along to the monastery.

But of course you have no idea what such a place is or where one might be, do you? Well, in the case of Rinzai, my own school of Buddhism, the place where you'll find the main practising monasteries is Kyoto, at the great Zen temples such as Tenryūji, Shōkokuji, Kenninji or others listed below.

Here is a list of monastery temples, divided into the three schools of Zen.

Rinzai: Buttsūji, Daitokuji, Eigenji, Engakuji, Hōkōji, Kenchōji, Kenninji, Kōgakuji, Kokutaiji, Myōshinji, Nanzenji, Shōkokuji, Tenryūji, Tōfukuji
Sōtō: Eiheiji, Sōjiji
Ōbaku: Manpukuji

The name Rinzai these days covers the various lineages of the fourteen temples listed here. The Sōtō school is represented by the great Eiheiji Temple in Fukui Prefecture and Sōjiji Temple in Yokohama. The smallest school, Ōbaku, is centred on Manpukuji Temple in Uji, near Kyoto.

Each of these head temples has a monastery directly attached to it.

A Typical Monastery Layout

This is the usual kind of layout

Chinjudō: often there are halls housing an image of bodhisattva Kannon, etc.

Inryō: this has the teacher's room, the *sanzen* room, etc.

Graves of past Zen masters

Toilet

Shoin: guest rooms
Kuri: office area
Tenzo: kitchen
Shokudō: dining hall
Yokusu: bath house etc.

Hondō: main hall, where sutras are chanted and ceremonies are conducted

Zendō: here the monks live and sit *zazen*

Shōdō (bell tower). This holds a large temple bell that is struck

Kyōdō (sutra hall). This houses a collection of sutras (Buddhist scriptures)

Sanmon (temple gate). Sometimes there's a paved path in front of this

21

In the case of the Rinzai and Sōtō schools, there are also monasteries in other areas that belong to that temple's lineage.

In the Rinzai school, the Myōshinji lineage is the largest. Apart from the monastery at Myōshinji itself, there are the monasteries of Shōfukuji in Fukuoka Prefecture, another of the same name in Kobe, Tokugenji in Nagoya, the Rinzai monastery in Shizuoka, Ryūtaku monastery in Mishima, and so on, making a total of eighteen regional monasteries. Besides these, the Nanzenji lineage has three, the Tōfukuji lineage has two, and the Daitokuji has one, though these numbers change from time to time for various reasons.

In order to become a priest of a local Rinzai Zen temple, you can study as a monk at any Rinzai-affiliated monastery. You can present yourself to any teacher you like, or simply choose a place that's geographically convenient for you. Or you could also decide to enter some monastery you know absolutely nothing about, in some far-off place.

Next I'll explain the structure of the Zen monastery. The illustration on the previous page shows the typical layout and buildings found in the monastery grounds.

The building where the monks live is called the *zendō* or meditation hall. The next illustration shows what it looks like inside. The floor is covered with tatami mats. Half a mat is just big enough for sitting *zazen*, and a whole mat is just big enough for sleeping on, which is the origin of the expression: 'Half-mat for waking, whole mat for sleeping'.

Let's Take a Look inside the Monastery

So just what kind of life do these Zen monks lead? Each monastery is a little different, but here is a typical daily schedule in a Rinzai monastery.

> 3 a.m. Rise. Sutra chanting in the main hall, followed by formal tea in the meditation hall, *zazen* meditation and *sanzen* meetings with the teacher.

The *Zendō*, Where the Monks Live

The layout of the *zendō* is extremely logical

A monk's 3 essential objects
- sutras
- eating implements
- tea cup

The monk's bedding is kept behind this curtain

Robe

Locker where he keeps his personal possessions

All a monk needs is a one-mat space for sleeping and a half-mat space for sitting

Senior monk with stick used to spur on the monk in his meditation

23

6 a.m. Breakfast.

7 a.m. Cleaning of main hall and meditation hall.

Remainder of the morning is spent in manual labour – outdoor cleaning, weeding, farm work, carpentry, etc., followed by *zazen* meditation.

1 p.m. Lunch.

Afternoon lecture on Zen given by the teacher. Manual labour. *Zazen* meditation.

4 p.m. Evening meal. Bath.

5 p.m. *Zazen* meditation and *sanzen*. Formal tea. *Zazen* meditation.

9 p.m. Lights out. Immediately after this, however, there is a review of the day's *zazen* meditation on the temple verandah. Monks usually get to bed at around midnight.

Formal tea in this case means a tea-drinking ceremony that follows a particular Zen ritual. The morning ceremony is for plum tea, a drink made by soaking a pickled plum in hot water, which clears the head. The evening ceremony is generally for Japanese tea and sweet bean cake. Tea is also served in the manual work period.

This routine is what occurs on normal days when nothing else is happening. Five or six times a month in the morning the monks leave the monastery to beg for alms. Seven or eight times a year there are intensive meditation sessions called *sesshin*. Besides these, there are fixed events on the temple calendar such as those at New Year, the spring and autumn equinoxes, and the mid-year Festival of the Dead.

Next let me describe what a monk wears.

There are basically four types of clothing worn by monks: everyday monk's robes (worn through three seasons), special summer robes, work clothes, and a sleeping robe (*zatsue*).

OK, now let's follow a basic version of a day in the life of a monk. See the illustration on page 28 for an explanation of the various gongs and bells mentioned here.

As you can see from the schedule above, the day starts early in a monastery.

Monks' Clothing Styles

Robes worn for Buddhist services
(dark blue cotton or black hemp in summer is best; synthetic is very hot)

Clothes for manual work
(synthetic or cotton; black, dark blue or grey)

Rakusu (simplest kind of surplice, worn for morning sutras and ceremonies)

Shusan

Cotton under-robe

Usually barefoot

sleeves and trouser hems gathered with elastic

Thick cotton work socks and split-toed heavy cloth shoes worn outside

Sleepwear
(cotton under-robe worn as underwear during the day)

It's hard to keep the hem neat

3 a.m. Suddenly in the darkness there comes the soft sound of a bell being rung in the main hall. This is a bell called a *shinrai*, for rousing people from their bed.

Then, from the meditation hall comes the sound of the *inkin* (a small bell struck with a metal stick) – *chin chichin chichichichi*.

Now the big gong answers from the main hall – *bong bong bong bong bong*.

No words are necessary in the monastery. All the signals are given using these various bells and gongs.

The next moment, the lights come on in the meditation hall and all the monks spring into action. It takes less than ten minutes to wash your face, use the toilet, get dressed and be seated.

Now the morning sutra service begins in the main hall. For about an hour the monks' voices are raised in chanting.

Next we all return to the meditation hall, drink our morning tea, and then meditate. As we sit there the sky slowly pales, and darkness gives way to light.

Then *don! don! don!* comes the beating of the wooden implement called the *moppan* that hangs at the entrance, echoing around the monastery. This sound signals the break of day.

And now the twittering of birds is heard. Yes, we live not just in a monastery but in the natural world, between the vast sky and the vast earth.

At the sounding of the gong known as the *kanshō*, breaking the quiet of the early morning, the monks all come running out. It's the time for the *sanzen* interview. They run twenty or thirty metres, then take their seats in a row. Silence descends again, as one by one the monks take turns to disappear into the *sanzen* room.

The interview with the teacher takes about three minutes, then the monk returns to the *zendō* to meditate.

6 o'clock is time for breakfast. This time a cloud-shaped drum called an *unban* is struck, the signal for the monks to proceed in ritual fashion to the refectory.

The breakfast menu is rice porridge and pickled plums, plus pickled white radish and seaweed simmered in soy sauce. The eating implements, called *jihatsu*, consist of a set of five bowls plus chopsticks and a wipe cloth and are a monk's personal equipment. The only words necessary during the meal are the chanting of sutras.

After breakfast the monks return to meditation, and immediately after that they clean the meditation hall. The only sounds to be heard are the sound of the monks pushing their cloths over the wooden floors, the cloths being wrung, and the swish of brooms.

Once the sound of footsteps has ceased, we enter the next round of meditation.

Now comes the sharp clack of the *taku* (wooden clappers). Then *ding ding ding ding*, the sound of the little *inkin*. With these four strikes, everything falls still. The meditation hall is hushed, except for the tiny occasional *plop* of incense ash falling. Time passes in a weighty silence, like time experienced deep beneath the sea.

Lunch is at 11 a.m. White rice plus a bowl of soup and another of vegetables – miso soup and boiled vegetables. It is eaten according to a set ritual, to the accompaniment of sutra chanting. The atmosphere is intense.

In the afternoon the teacher gives a lecture on Zen. The topic is *kōans*, but this is a general commentary on them and of course the answers are not provided. After around an hour, there is more meditation.

The evening meal is at 4 p.m. It consists of a stew made from the leftovers from the earlier meals. A bowl of this is served to the accompaniment of sutra chanting. The monks sitting there mutely eating are bathed in the soft light of a dimly glowing naked light bulb.

Once the meal is over, the time for the bath is upon us without a moment to draw breath.

A short time later the monks walk softly back to the meditation hall.

Now the great bell in the bell tower is struck, and the designated monk chants a sutra. As soon as this is over comes the beating of the *moppan* to signal the sunset.

Soon, the meditation hall is shrouded in darkness. The only sounds are the clack of the *taku* and the ringing of the *inkin*, repeated alternately to signal the beginning and end of the meditation session.

Bong bong bong bong goes the *kanshō* bell, signalling the second *sanzen* interviews of the day.

Out rush the monks with a great clatter. Then one by one they return to the meditation hall, and silence reigns once more.

The Main Instruments Rung in the Monastery
All activities are signalled by sounds

Waking: *shinrai*
(the day begins)

Time signals: *moppan*
(struck at dawn and dusk)

Zazen: *taku*

Inkin

(signals beginning and end
of meditation sessions)

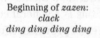

Beginning of *zazen*:
clack
ding ding ding ding

End of *zazen*:
ding
clack clack

Sanzen: *kanshō*
(struck when entering
sanzen room)

Meals: *unban*
(signals the beginning
of a meal)

After tea and sweet bean cake comes the *ding ding ding* of the little *inkin* bell signalling the start of another meditation session.

Then at 9 o'clock the wooden *moppan* is struck to signal the time for lights out.

Now the monks chant sutras, lay out their bedding, and the lights of the meditation hall go out. But they don't sleep yet. Still to come is the 'night sitting' on the verandah of the main hall. There in the moonlight, beneath the star-filled sky, the monks forget time as they sit on in meditation.

So there you are. The monastery is a man's world.

Do all the monks spend their time from dawn to dusk in meditation? No. The monastery consists of monks who spend most of their time meditating, doing manual work and begging, and other resident monks who see to the business side of the running of the monastery. The exact organization differs from one temple to another and depending on the number of monks, but here's a general summary of how it works. First, the group whose life centres on meditation, manual work and begging:

Jikijitsu: The highest position after the teacher. General monastery supervisor. The role of a senior monk.

Jishiki: Meditation hall attendant, who ensures that the various activities all go smoothly.

Jokei: Junior officer under the *Jikijitsu*. In charge of educating new monks. Usually very strict, like the worst kind of sergeant major.

Shintō: (Not a job description.) The name of monks in their first year at the monastery. Those in their second year are called 'Old *Shintō*'.

The group of resident monks who conduct the administration of the monastery (each has an individual room):

Shika: Responsible for the monastery overall. Ensures that the teacher's intentions are reflected in what happens in the monastery.

Tenzo: Head cook for the monastery. Acquires food supplies, cooks meals and clears up.

Fūsu: Monastery accountant. Creates and controls the account books that form the basis for the documentation submitted to the tax office.

Fuzui: The monk who looks after financial affairs and organizes general provisions for the monastery.

Densu: Responsible for leading sutra chanting and rituals. He also has the job of waking the monks in the morning.

Inji: The teacher's attendant, who looks after his needs.

When you first enter the monastery, the teacher gives you the name you will be known by there. My name became Genryū (the literal meaning is something like Profound Dragon). From the tradition of using the second part of a monk's name as a kind of nickname, I was generally referred to as Ryū-san, but when you're assigned a post you are referred to by its title – Jikijitsu-san, Jokei-san, Tenzo-san, etc.

April and October are the seasons for re-assigning roles, and I was always eager to find out what new role I would be given. One of my favourite jobs was the role of head cook or *tenzo*, which I'll talk about in more detail in Chapter 3.

Zazen Meditation

A Three-Minute Zazen *Lecture*

I can't talk about life in the monastery without discussing *zazen* meditation, of course.

So first let's sit and cross our legs.

You put your right foot on your left thigh, then your left foot over it onto your right thigh. You can also do this with opposite feet. This position, the full lotus position, is called *kekka fuza*.

For those people who think, 'Ouch! I can't get my foot up there!', you can just put one foot on your thigh. This is the half-lotus position, called *hanka fuza*.

The Main Points for *Zazen* Meditation

Method of breathing
• Breathe slowly and deeply through your nose
• Count your breaths

Hands form the cosmic *mudra*
• Rest the left hand in the right
• A slight space is left between the thumbs

How to fold your legs

Half-closed eyes
• Lower the gaze about 45 degrees to rest approximately one metre in front of you

Straighten your spine

Meditation cushion (*zafu*)

Cushion base

Full lotus (lifting both feet)

Half lotus (lifting one foot)

Cushion and base

The illustration features the essential points for *zazen* sitting. The five points are:

1. Fold your legs.
2. Straighten your spine.
3. Place your hands in the cosmic *mudra* position.

4. Half close your eyes and focus about a metre in front of you.
5. Breathe in the *zazen* way (abdominal breathing).

The breath is slow and deep, characterized by a complete exhalation before the next inhalation. When you first enter the monastery you learn to master the observation of breath by counting your exhalations. This technique allows you to avoid distracting thoughts.

I remember a time not long after I became a monk. Whenever I sat *zazen* under my teacher Sōchū, he would always say, 'Are you counting?'

'Yes, I'm counting,' I'd reply. Then one day I said instead, 'Yes, I'm at two hundred and thirty-five.'

The teacher laughed. 'Look, what you do is count to ten and then go back to one again,' he explained.

That's the normal method for observing your breath.

Remember the old teacher who explained how to avoid being bitten by mosquitoes? He once said to me, 'Don't forget, you mustn't pay too much attention to the numbers when you're counting your breaths. If you find yourself too caught up in the counting you should just meditate by thinking "*mu*" with every out breath.'

Mu is the word we saw in Chapter 1 in the *kōan* about the dog and Buddha nature. It's a deep meditation tool, but of course just saying '*mu*' doesn't necessarily get you there. Anyway, this technique of observing the breath by counting is an important one in *zazen* meditation.

OK, let's just try it for three minutes.

If you can't get into the half-lotus position you can sit on your knees, or even on a chair.

.... (1 minute)
.... (2 minutes)
.... (3 minutes)

Three minutes is the time it takes to wait for instant noodles to be ready, or for Ultraman to pull off his stunts, but I'm guessing it felt amazingly long for you just now.

So what sounds did you hear during those three minutes?

Birdsong perhaps? The sound of the wind? Perhaps the sound of rain? Or if you're in a town you may have heard the sound of cars going by.

But these aren't sounds you only heard during those three minutes, you know. You were hearing them all along. It's just that you weren't aware of them.

Registering and observing with your eyes and ears these things that were there all along is where *zazen* meditation begins from.

I remember my first *sesshin* in the monastery – *sesshin* is the name for the week-long intensive of day and night *zazen* periods. On about day four, I was aware that I was mentally and physically settling into the *sesshin*. Your five senses – eyes, ears, nose, mouth and skin – become more sensitive. Air tastes like air, water tastes like water. On my third *sesshin* I remember I breathed the scent of moisture in the air and thought to myself, 'Hmm, I wonder if that's rain on the way', and sure enough a little while later came the sound of rain pattering on the roof.

I said above that feeling and observing with your senses is where *zazen* starts from, but it's hard to express how sharpened your senses become in a *sesshin*. I could say that your sense of self-existence – where you were born, for instance, what you've done until now, and what you plan to do in the future – seems to fade into transparency with each new breath. You're aware of becoming one with the air around you, aware of the sounds of wind and rain, the song of birds and insects, all passing straight through you. I really can't explain it very well. It seems to me that *zazen* opens up for you a world beyond the reach of language.

A Schoolteacher and His Student Visit the Monastery

Here's a little story about *zazen*.

One December a teacher from a nearby high school – in the next town, as I recall – brought a student along to do some *zazen*.

Now it's a bit strange for a student to come along to the monastery like this outside the normal times of the spring and summer holidays. You can pretty much guess what's going on, and this case was no exception. This young fellow, let's call him A, had been causing trouble at school and his punishment was to come to the monastery for three days. The teacher was there to accompany him. The teacher must have been in his late forties. He was a bit on the plump side, and wore a navy blue suit with a little string tie. Young A, on the other hand, dressed in a black school uniform, was pale and spindly and rather timid-looking. On the first day, when they were about to begin monastic life, the teacher turned to the student and said with a deeply earnest expression, 'Now you sit there and meditate hard and contemplate yourself, OK? If you get through the next three days and do everything properly, we'll allow you to come back to school.'

And so began the brief but lengthy period of monastic life on which the student's return to school depended.

Clack! went the wooden clappers, signalling the start of meditation in the *zendō*.

When he first settled down to meditate the teacher sat there with a strained look on his face that proclaimed how intensely he was concentrating, but within barely five minutes his brow had furrowed and a pained expression had settled on his features. His legs were hurting.

Young A, on the other hand, gave absolutely no sign of enthusiasm for the task, but neither did he look particularly uncomfortable.

Four o'clock arrived – meal time. The food was a dish of rice porridge.

The teacher sat gazing into his bowl, and his disappointment was plain to see. Slowly he picked up his chopsticks, then he stirred the contents of the bowl just for a final check and heaved a small sigh. There wasn't so much as a shellfish to give it any real substance. Finally, gloomily, he began to sip the plain gruel.

Meanwhile young A had already tucked in, without enthusiasm as usual but with a little shrug that said, 'OK. Whatever.'

Once the meal was over it was back to *zazen* again.

It was chilly December, and there was not so much as a hint of heating in the meditation hall. What's more the windows were wide

34

Don't come to a monastery in winter!

open, which meant that the winter wind blew straight in. The teacher sat there huddled like a crouching cat, and from time to time a shiver ran through him.

Then came a toilet break, and the teacher reached thoughtlessly for a cigarette.

'No smoking!' bellowed the monk in charge.

You should have seen young A's delight! For once he beamed from ear to ear, full of youthful joy, all his listlessness forgotten.

Next morning at 3 a.m. the meditation hall was cold as ice. If you breathed deeply you could fend off the worst of the cold, but the teacher of course didn't know the technique of meditation breathing and he sat there getting no warmer.

The time came to eat the 6 a.m. morning rice porridge, and after he had downed it the teacher spoke up. 'Er, actually you know, I think this is all a bit too harsh for educational purposes. Perhaps it's time to leave now if you don't mind.' And with that he departed.

And young A? 'Well, if the teacher's leaving I guess I should leave too,' he said as he turned to go. 'Can't be helped. I have to do whatever he says.'

If you're as young and strong as a high school student you can cope with life in the monastery. But if you're over forty it's a different story!

It's best to go while you're in your twenties. It's not exactly baseball, but with youth and vigour on your side you can get a certain enjoyment out of living in a monastery.

The Secrets of *Takuhatsu*, the Skill of *Samu*

The Kitten in the Alms Bag

Here I'll talk about the monastic begging known as *takuhatsu*, and the monastic manual labour known as *samu*.

I imagine most people would think of meditation when they think of monastic practice. And if it's the Rinzai school, you'd probably also think of *kōans*. But begging rounds and physical labour are also an important part of a monk's practice.

Almost all the Rinzai monasteries beg for alms five or six times a month. The time and day as well as the route for these begging rounds are predetermined, and usually the monks set off in a group.

When I was in the monastery we used to set out at 7.30 a.m., and from around 8 till noon we would follow a set course through the neighbourhood streets.

There are two basic methods. In one, the monks pause at every door, chant a sutra and beg for alms. In the other they don't chant sutras but simply walk through the streets loudly intoning a cry – '*Hō-ō! hō-ō!*' (pronounced as a drawn out 'haw').

Hō is the word for 'law', meaning the Buddhist Law or teachings. According to one theory, it means 'the raining down of the Law', i.e. the Buddhist Law is raining down over all.

Apparently, some women who lived in our begging area didn't hear this cry of ours as *hō-ō* but as *aw-aw*, and they used to warn their children, 'If you don't do as you're told the *Aw-aw* Man will come and take you away!' The kids would shiver with fear and beg to be spared, and promise meekly to do everything they should.

Mind you, I'm pretty sure this scare tactic wouldn't work for a child above six or seven.

Going Begging

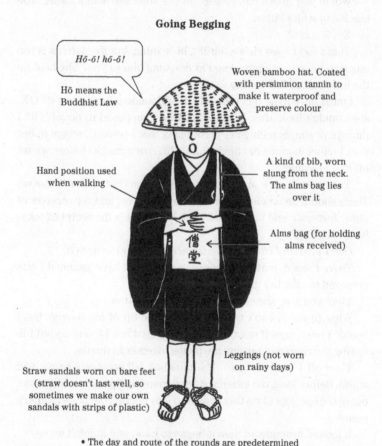

Hō-ō! hō-ō!

Hō means the Buddhist Law

Woven bamboo hat. Coated with persimmon tannin to make it waterproof and preserve colour

Hand position used when walking

A kind of bib, worn slung from the neck. The alms bag lies over it

Alms bag (for holding alms received)

Leggings (not worn on rainy days)

Straw sandals worn on bare feet (straw doesn't last well, so sometimes we make our own sandals with strips of plastic)

• The day and route of the rounds are predetermined
• Numbers of monks per group and details of the practice vary by monastery

Anyway, let's take a look at what a begging monk looks like. In the Rinzai sect, monks wear a kind of bag hung around the neck, into which they put the various things they are given as alms.

One day, not long after I'd entered the monastery, I was walking through the streets begging for alms when a middle-aged woman popped out of her house and called me over.

'Would you take a cat, please.' In her arms she held a sweet little black-and-white kitten.

'Er . . . a cat?'

'That's right, yes. He's a darling little thing, but five kittens is too much to keep in the house so I'm donating him to you.' She held up the little ball of fluff for me to see.

I must have looked completely dumbfounded. I mean, a cat? OK, she couldn't look after it, but what was *I* supposed to do with it? I thought of simply telling her point-blank that I couldn't accept it, but then I remembered what Sōchū had told us new monks before we set off that morning:

'You mustn't pick and choose what you accept with *takuhatsu*. There should be no distinction between the giver and the receiver of alms. Just walk and breathe with the *hō-ō*. This is the secret of *takuhatsu* begging.'

Don't pick and choose. No distinctions, I said to myself.

There I stood, making no move, so she must have assumed I was prepared to take her gift.

'Here you are,' she said, and held out the kitten.

What to do? 'I can't take it,' was on the tip of my tongue, but I couldn't bring myself to say it. Unable to resist her, I found myself following the rules and putting my palms together in thanks.

Then off I walked again. My alms bag felt strangely heavy and warm. Before long, the kitten wriggled round and poked its little head out of the bag, just like a tiny kangaroo joey peering out of its mother's pouch.

It looked around and then it began to mew, and it didn't let up.

'You wouldn't like being in a bag like this either!' it seemed to be saying.

I stroked its soft little head. And then the kitten began to lick my finger. Its rough little tongue was quite a surprise for me.

I grew more and more gloomy. What on earth was I going to do

The Monk's Alms Bag

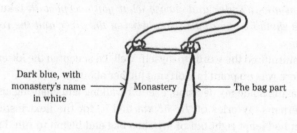

Dark blue, with monastery's name in white → Monastery ← The bag part

Correct way to perform *takuhatsu*

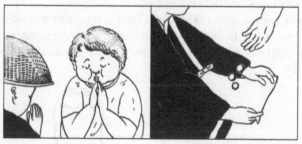

1. Palms together

2. Receive alms in outstretched alms bag

3. Tip alms into bag

4. Palms together once again

with a cat? I should have just said no. What would they say when I got back to the temple?

But the teacher himself had told me the key to correct *takuhatsu*, and it was because I'd stood there recalling his words that I'd found myself in this fix.

You mustn't pick and choose what you accept with takuhatsu. *There should be no distinction between the giver and the receiver of alms.*

I murmured the words to myself. Well, I'd accepted the kitten now, so there was no point in worrying further about it.

Having made my decision, I set off walking and chanting again.

Perhaps my cries of '*Hō-ō!*' startled it, for the next instant the kitten had leapt right out of my alms bag and begun to run. I set off after it, but it ducked swiftly round a corner and disappeared, perhaps into someone's garden.

To be honest, one of the feelings I had at this point was relief. The kitten was gone. But even more than relief was a deep concern, and also a dislike of myself for having been in two minds about keeping

Tea cup. When not in use, wrapped in cloth and stored on the shelf behind you.

Cloth

Rice cake eaten with tea. Can also be bean-paste bread, melon pastry or other sweet.

Platform

it. If the teacher had found out about the incident, I think this is the thing he would have been most critical of.

For a while after that, every time I was out on *takuhatsu* begging rounds I was haunted by the thought of that black-and-white kitten, recalling the feel of its strange warm weight inside my alms bag.

Here's another *takuhatsu* episode I recall.

One day I stopped to beg in front of a bakery and a pretty young girl came out to greet me.

New to this experience, she asked what she should do.

'If you'd like to give alms, I can receive whatever you care to give,' I explained.

'Would bread be OK?'

'Yes.'

'Right, then please take whatever you want.'

She took me inside and I chose a bag of the free items on offer that day – bean paste buns, cream buns and the like.

Later that day these buns turned up as our tea cakes. It's wrong to pick and choose on *takuhatsu*, as we all know, but in this case the story was a happy one for everyone.

I have to confess that not only were the buns a pleasure to receive but I also took secret pleasure in the chance to meet this girl.

Autumn deepened, and one day when I went to call at the bakery on my *takuhatsu* rounds I found that not only the girl but the bakery itself had disappeared. Where it had stood was now just empty ground.

A chill autumn wind sang in the air, piercing my heart to the quick, and I felt the figure of that smiling, long-haired girl swirling up and flying away with it. Her smile trembled and grew distant until it was lost to sight.

I don't need to tell you how disappointed I was at my discovery.

Another kind of *takuhatsu* is the so-called 'distant *takuhatsu*' known as *enpatsu*. With *enpatsu*, you go somewhere further than usual from the monastery, and perform *takuhatsu* for several days, sleeping over.

Then there's also what's known as *daikonhatsu*, in which the monastery receives in winter the pickled *daikon* (white radish) essential for all three meals.

The Secrets of Monastery Cleaning

Now let's look at *samu*.

This is what the manual labour performed in the monastery is called. There are various kinds – cleaning, wood-chopping, field work and monastery repairs.

The most popular, though, is cleaning. That's because it's a daily task to keep the grounds and the buildings such as the main hall and the meditation hall clean.

I'll pass on to you the secrets of monastery cleaning. The rules are detailed, right down to the way you hold the wash cloth against the floorboards.

1. Buckets, brooms, wash cloths and other cleaning implements are kept in neat order in the right place. There is no piling them up in any old order, or changing the place where they're kept.
2. Water for the buckets is recycled water from the bath. Buckets are filled to 10 centimetres below the rim.

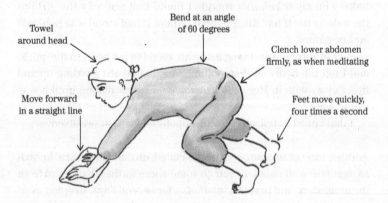

Towel around head

Bend at an angle of 60 degrees

Clench lower abdomen firmly, as when meditating

Move forward in a straight line

Feet move quickly, four times a second

3. Wash cloths are first tightly wrung out. When cleaning the wooden floor with a wash cloth, you stand and bend forward at an angle of sixty degrees, hold the cloth against the floor and move it in rhythm with the same abdominal breathing used in meditation. You must be careful not to leave anywhere unwiped, paying particular attention to the edges.

4. You don't throw away the dirty water but pour it around the trees and plants to nurture them.

The order of monastery cleaning is also fixed. You must start at a certain place and end at a certain place, following a predetermined route. You can't get away with deciding from day to day where to start and finish.

The *samu* that I was fondest and proudest of was cleaning. Working in the fields wasn't too bad. I was pretty good at harvesting potatoes, putting them into boxes and transporting them to the monastery in a little truck. It was carpentry that I had most trouble with. When repairs were needed in the monastery, we assisted the carpenter by carrying the materials or digging holes, but this was tough for me as I was rather a weakling.

One unfortunate day, I was ordered by one of my seniors to climb onto the roof. Up the ladder I went. So far so good, but once there I froze. It was all I could do to simply lie spread out like a lizard, clinging to the tiles for dear life.

'Hey, what do you think you're doing?' yelled another senior monk. 'You're getting in the way! Come down and work on the ground!'

True, I was no use just lying there on the roof hanging on. I could only get in the way. But when I went to do as told and come down, I found I couldn't. I was OK climbing up the ladder, but my feet refused to climb down.

In the end, my day's *samu* was entirely taken up with climbing up to the roof and somehow making my way down again.

This episode became the talk of the monastery, and from then on I did my best to be inconspicuous whenever there was repair work to be done. Mind you, I don't think this was really necessary – I can't imagine that anyone would have ordered me up on a roof again anyway.

OK, that's enough of my tales of failure. So what is the secret of *samu*? Well, in a word it's to perform it wholeheartedly. If you're cleaning with a wash cloth, just clean. If you're working in the field, just do field work. If you're helping with repair work, focus on that work and do it with all your heart. That's the secret of *samu*.

The same thing can be said of *takuhatsu*. Don't think about irrelevant things, just get on with doing what you're doing.

The root of this is the *zazen* concept of 'becoming each breath'. Let me put it this way – in *zazen* we control body, mind and breath together, while in *takuhatsu* and *samu* we add the physical movements of real life to this experience.

3

There's Nothing Like Zen for being Food-Fussy

An ABC of Zen Food

Kitchen Work is Another Kind of Zen Practice

After I'd left the monastery, when the time had come to marry, I did what used to be common in Japan in those days – I had an arranged meeting with a young woman who'd been selected as a potential wife for me, to see if we liked each other. While we chatted, she remarked with a smile that she knew nothing about cooking.

'Eh?'

'Well, my mother's always done the cooking for me, right through from when I was a student to now when I work in an office. What about you?'

'Well, I've lived in a monastery so I can cook reasonably well.'

'But surely you don't always eat Zen vegetarian cuisine?'

'No, once we've left the monastery men like me who live in normal temples eat food just like other families.'

'That's a relief. So what about housework and clothes washing and so on?'

'I can probably do all that as well as the average housewife.'

'Wow, that's wonderful!'

I'm not sure just what was so wonderful, but apparently this is now an age when a man's ability to cook, clean and wash could be considered a qualification for marriage.

*

As a general rule, anyone who spends time in a monastery learns to look after the everyday things of life for himself. No one else is going to do it for you, after all. You learn how to cook. As I said in the last chapter, we take turns in the various roles, and everyone gets a turn at being head cook. In the Zen world, the head cook is called the *tenzo*. Once you're given the role of *tenzo*, you spend every day for six months preparing food, cooking, clearing up and cleaning the kitchen. The essential menu (in the case of Rinzai monasteries) is as follows:

Morning: Thin rice porridge, pickled plums, a side dish (kelp simmered in soy, for example), pickled white radish.

Midday: A bowl of soup and a vegetable dish (rice plus miso soup plus boiled vegetables is considered one dish), pickled white radish.

Evening: Thick rice porridge (the day's leftovers cooked up together), a side dish (spinach cooked in a soy sauce dressing, for example), pickled white radish.

Really? you might say. If that's all you have to do, just cook and clean up, I do that every day too! What's the big deal about it being a Zen practice?

Actually, cooking is a wonderful form of practice, and what's more it's difficult in a different way from meditation. On the one hand there's the sheer skill involved in slicing vegetables, boiling, grilling, and adjusting the taste. But the most difficult part of being *tenzo* lies in the task of intuitively grasping how to bring out the essential life of the things you cook, and how this in turn brings life to those who eat it.

So how do you actually go about doing this? Here in a nutshell are the basic teachings on this:

1. Use everything and throw away nothing.
2. Cook according to the taste of those who will eat it.
3. Accept it all with gratitude.

The details of these rules can be found in the great Zen teacher Dōgen's instructions on the art of monastic cooking, titled *Tenzo kyōkun* (*The*

Tenzo Precepts, 1237), but I think the above three points are a fair summary in present-day form.

If you leave rice and vegetables, they spoil. The life of food should be treated with the same care as our own life, and used to its maximum potential. This is the meaning of point 1 above – use everything and throw away nothing.

Point 2 – cook according the taste of those who will eat it – means that you should create the food for the sake of your companions who've been dedicating themselves to the hard work of meditation, rather than making it to suit your own taste.

Particular care should be taken during the intensive meditation sessions. As I said before, around the third day of intensive sitting, one's eyes, nose, taste buds and ears become hyper-sensitive. You need to take this into account and slowly reduce the amount of food as well as refining the flavour so that it doesn't interfere with meditation.

This is *shōjin ryōri*, Zen vegetarian food. We are imbibing the life force in the vegetables, seaweed and fruit we eat, so it's essential to chant a sutra and 'accept it all with gratitude', point number 3 above. This means to eat with an attitude of humble thanks rather than just gobbling the food down.

Some monastery kitchens these days make use of modern equipment such as gas cookers, while others stick to the old ways and still use firewood for cooking.

Everyone will have some problems with being *tenzo* in the beginning . . .

'I'm way behind with preparing the midday meal because I took too long peeling the potatoes!'

'Oops, I've added too much soy sauce!'

'Oh no! Now I've gone and burned the pot!'

And so on. It's a bit like the Japanese saying, 'You learn sumo wrestling through losing.' We learn to cook through a process of endless scoldings from the teacher and other monks, and endless mistakes.

Welcome to a Monastery-style Menu

Let me introduce a few menus typical of monastery meals.

Let's start with pickled white radish *Tsukudani* (which means simmered in soy).

1. Slice the pickled white radish thinly, place in a bowl and rinse out the excess salt under running water.
2. Cook it down in a saucepan until it's reduced to a paste.
3. Add soy sauce and sugar to taste.

It's more or less the same process as when you make a *tsukudani* of *nori* seaweed. Another similar dish is tea *tsukudani*, where you gather up the tea leaves left in the teapot, boil them down to a paste and add soy sauce and sugar as above. If you toss this tea *tsukudani* together with leftover rice and vegetables in a pan, you create what's known as tea rice, *nichijō sahanji*, a phrase which also means 'something commonplace or everyday'. As to the taste, well . . . with the best will in the world I couldn't call it delicious, but it's worth trying if you're interested.

Next let's try bamboo shoot.

In the balmy season of May when bamboo shoots begin to appear, in our monastery there used to be a run of days when a set meal of bamboo shoot was served. This was bamboo shoot rice with a clear bamboo shoot soup and boiled fresh bamboo shoot accompaniment.

To make boiled fresh bamboo shoot:

1. Coarsely chop the boiled bamboo shoot and fry it in oil.
2. Cut *wakame* seaweed into fine threads, mix with the bamboo, and boil until the *wakame* becomes viscous.
3. Adjust the flavour with soy sauce and sesame oil.

The key is to reduce the *wakame* to a viscous paste. It takes a bit of time, so if you're cooking at home it might be easiest to put it through a blender. The result is delicious. I haven't once made the tea *tsukudani*

How to Make Boiled Fresh Bamboo Shoot

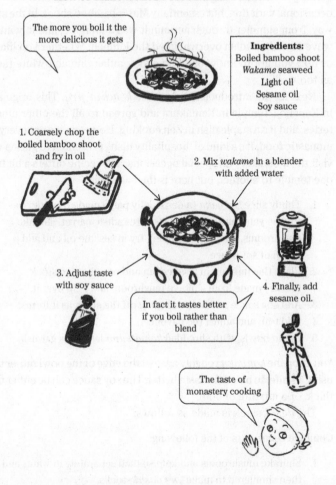

The more you boil it the more delicious it gets

Ingredients:
Boiled bamboo shoot
Wakame seaweed
Light oil
Sesame oil
Soy sauce

1. Coarsely chop the boiled bamboo shoot and fry in oil

2. Mix *wakame* in a blender with added water

3. Adjust taste with soy sauce

4. Finally, add sesame oil.

In fact it tastes better if you boil rather than blend

The taste of monastery cooking

dish I described earlier since I left the monastery, but I make this one every May in bamboo shoot season.

In the monastery, though, I didn't find this dish very pleasant. Behind our temple there was a hill covered in bamboo where you could dig endless shoots in May, so every day for as long as they kept coming we kept eating this set bamboo shoot meal. There was an occasional variation, but essentially May = bamboo shoot. In the same way, from summer through autumn it was aubergine, and in winter a wave of white radish overwhelmed the kitchen. Whether you liked it or not, you got to know bamboo shoot, aubergine and white radish all too well!

Next let me introduce a dish called *kenchin-jiru*. This originated in Kenchōji Temple in Kamakura and spread to all the other monasteries, and it's a staple dish in Zen cooking. However, it's not everyday monastic food. It's a kind of 'hospitality dish', presented to guests who visit the monastery on special occasions. The recipe differs a bit from one temple to another, but here is the basic one:

1. Thinly slice *konyaku* (a dense jelly paste made from devil's tongue yam) and vegetables (white radish, carrot, shiitake mushrooms, taro, for example), fry in sesame oil and add a touch of soy sauce.
2. Place this mixture in a saucepan and pour boiling stock (*dashi*) made from shiitake mushroom and kelp over it.
3. Add soy sauce and boil, scooping off the scum as it forms.
4. Add tofu and adjust the flavour.
5. Put in bowls, with shredded *komatsuna* leaves as garnish.

You chop the *konyaku* roughly against the edge of the bowl rather than using a knife, to blend the taste better. The soy sauce can be either thin, thick, or a mixture of both.

The *dashi* stock is made as follows:

Combine equal parts of the following:

1. Shiitake mushrooms and kelp soaked separately in water and then simmered to make two *dashi* stocks.
2. Rice water from rinsing white rice (the second rinse, not the first), boiled.

The key to a good *kenchin-jiru* is not to serve it right away but to leave it for half a day to let the flavour develop, and then reheat.

How to Make *Kenchin-jiru*

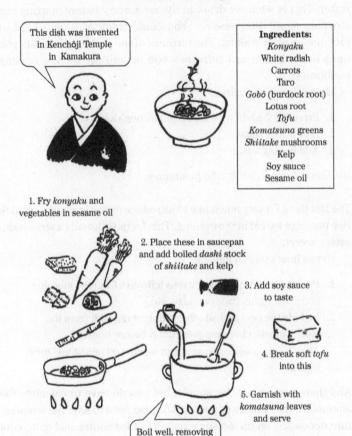

This dish was invented in Kenchōji Temple in Kamakura

Ingredients:
Konyaku
White radish
Carrots
Taro
Gobō (burdock root)
Lotus root
Tofu
Komatsuna greens
Shiitake mushrooms
Kelp
Soy sauce
Sesame oil

1. Fry *konyaku* and vegetables in sesame oil

2. Place these in saucepan and add boiled *dashi* stock of *shiitake* and kelp

3. Add soy sauce to taste

4. Break soft *tofu* into this

5. Garnish with *komatsuna* leaves and serve

Boil well, removing floating foam

Just by the way, there's also a dish called *kokushō-jiru*, made like *kenchin-jiru* but with miso replacing the soy sauce. This one originated in the Kokushōji Temple in Shizuoka Prefecture, a Rinzai Zen temple belonging to the Engakuji school.

*

The next dish I'll introduce is called *baitō*, pickled plum in hot water. This is what we drink in the monastery before starting our morning meditation session. You could think of it as a kind of pick-me-up after waking. The tartness of the pickled plum hits you deep down inside and refreshes you beautifully for the coming meditation.

Here's how you make it:

1. Press the flesh of a pickled plum through a sieve.
2. Add a little sugar.
3. Add boiling water.

It's also delicious drunk cold in summer.

The last thing I'd very much like to introduce to you is *zōsui*, the thick rice porridge we eat in the evening. This recipe is usually a strict monastery secret.

Here's how you can make it.

1. Put into a saucepan the various leftovers from the morning and noon meals (rice porridge, etc.).
2. Include the peel and all other edible scraps left from the earlier meals, chopping them finely before boiling.
3. After heating, add soy sauce and sesame oil or salt and miso to taste.

And there you have it. It's simple, but you do have to calculate the amount for the number of people. You also need to alter the temperature depending on the season – piping hot for winter, and quite cool in the summer months.

It's said that back in the days of the Buddha, monks only ate one meal a day and nothing after midday. When Buddhism arrived in China this got expanded to two meals a day, and this custom was continued in Japan until around the thirteenth century. The origin of the evening meal is said to have been the need for extra sustenance in very cold and snowy areas. In other words, the evening meal started as a kind of extra to the monastery meals. But the evening *zōsui* that I've just described is actually the meal that brings out the best in the cook. In my opinion, it's the ultimate monastery food.

No matter how you try to use every bit of the ingredients, there will often be some vegetable matter you need to throw out. We don't waste that in the monastery either. We mix it with fallen leaves and soil and use it as compost to fertilize the vegetable garden. These days everyone's talking about recycling, but temple monasteries have been doing it for hundreds of years.

Respecting Food Etiquette is Also a Form of Zen Practice

Table Manners in the Monastery

It's not just cooking. Zen is also fussy about eating. This goes for Dōgen, founder of the Sōtō school of Zen, too.

Dōgen wrote a great number of works besides his famous *Shōbōgenzō*. One of them is called *Eihei daishinsa*. It's essentially a rule book for life in the monastery at Eiheiji Temple, which he founded.

One of the chapters concerns food, and it opens with these words: 'One who is correct in eating follows the Buddha in all ways. One who follows the Buddha in all ways is also correct in eating.'

Having established this fundamental relationship between food etiquette and right living, *Eihei daishinsa* goes on to describe in detail how to enter the eating hall, how to handle your eating utensils, and the correct table manners for the beginning, middle and end of a meal. There are quite a few bits that can make a reader chuckle.

Don't dig straight into the middle of the dish.
Don't request different food on the excuse of some passing illness.
Don't hide food under your rice and then claim you weren't given it.
Don't look at the bowl of the fellow beside you and get upset that
he got more than you did.

Reading these things reminded me of meal times in primary school, when we'd quarrel about who got more than whom.

'Hey, you gave him more! That's not fair!'

'I didn't get any meat in my curry!'

'Favouritism!'

Sometimes there were so many complaints that the teachers and servers had a hard time keeping everyone happy.

Dōgen's advice still rings true today:

> Don't roll your rice into a ball to eat it.
>
> Don't eat noisily.
>
> Don't wave your hands around while eating.
>
> Don't eat leaning forward with your elbows resting on your knees.
>
> Don't spread the rice around with your hand.
>
> Don't heap the rice up into a mountain.
>
> Don't mix the other food in with the rice.
>
> Don't stuff your cheeks full like a monkey.

I remember in our primary school there would be a 'Rule of the Day', such as not to chatter or not to walk around during class. Of course this implies that we kids did a lot of these things. So we can imagine from the above rule that in Dōgen's day there were monks who actually ate like monkeys.

Here are a few more of his reprimands:

> Don't drool in anticipation while you're waiting for another helping.
>
> Don't scratch your head while you're eating.
>
> Don't sway from side to side, hug your knees, stand up on your knees, stretch or yawn.
>
> Don't blow your nose and make a weird noise.

His rules can be bizarrely detailed. The monks in modern monasteries are all in their late teens or twenties, so some of these rules sound very odd if applied to them. But quite young boys became monks back then, and it's likely that such rules were addressed to them.

Behind Dōgen's rules we can see that table manners in Dōgen's day were probably very rough and ready. In another text, he lamented, 'There is complete ignorance of the fact that rules for cooking and eating are part of the Buddhist Way; monks are just like animals.'

This is what lies behind his strict attempts to set high standards around food. This diligence and devotion (*shōjin*) lie at the heart of Zen food (*shōjin ryōri*) today.

Be Quick and Set Out the Bowls!

So what's happened to this table etiquette in monasteries today?

There are differences in rules and utensils between the two Zen sects, Rinzai and Sōtō, but in both sects the rules are very precise.

In my early days in the monastery I was so stressed I never felt I'd actually eaten after I'd had a meal.

Each monk carries his own set of five eating bowls, called *jihatsu*, and the rules for handling them are extremely complex.

Not only is it tricky to set out your bowls correctly, but while you do it you're chanting sutras and being served, and it's all so complex that you can get quite panicky. What's more, there are small differences in the sutras you chant at breakfast and lunch, and the novice monk hasn't yet learned the sutras by heart so he has to read and turn the pages as he chants.

And just when you're engrossed in the chanting, an older monk will bark, 'Be quick and set out the bowls!'

You pause in the chanting to get your bowls right, and now you hear a rain of reprimands.

'Concentrate on your chanting!'

'Memorize the sutra, you fool!'

'Hey, stop dreaming. You're being served!'

When your turn comes to be served rice, it's the practice to acknowledge it by placing the palms of your hands together, *gasshō* style. But you have to be careful.

'Ooof!' Before you know it your bowl is being crammed with a mountain of rice. You have to learn that in the monastery it's the custom to wordlessly indicate with your hands how much you want.

The Monk's Utensils

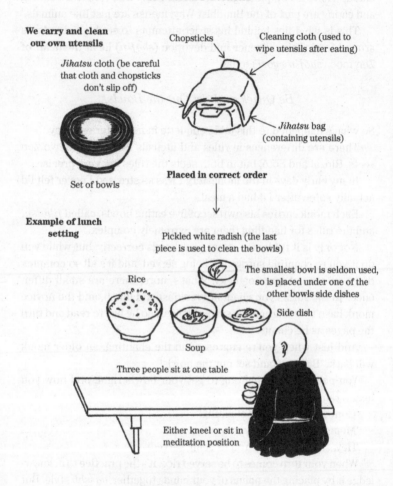

**We carry and clean
our own utensils**

Chopsticks

Cleaning cloth (used to
wipe utensils after eating)

Jihatsu cloth (be careful
that cloth and chopsticks
don't slip off)

Jihatsu bag
(containing utensils)

Set of bowls

Placed in correct order

**Example of lunch
setting**

Pickled white radish (the last
piece is used to clean the bowls)

The smallest bowl is seldom used,
so is placed under one of the
other bowls side dishes

Rice

Side dish

Soup

Three people sit at one table

Either kneel or sit in
meditation position

Rules for use differ slightly between
monasteries and depending on meals

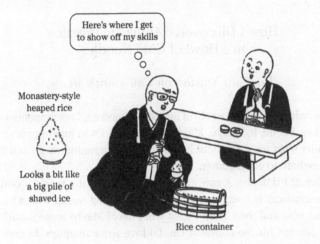

Here's where I get to show off my skills

Monastery-style heaped rice

Looks a bit like a big pile of shaved ice

Rice container

Drawing a little circle with your two palms tells the server that he's giving you more than enough, while softly sliding your palms off each other means 'Stop'.

So if you simply put your hands together in the normal way you'll find yourself landed with a great heap of rice in your bowl, and what's more there's no way to return it to the serving dish. You just have to force down this towering mountain of rice, like it or not.

Not only is eating etiquette complex, but if you're a designated server things get even more tricky.

There are differences in the basic rules for serving rice at breakfast, lunch and dinner, and the rules also change depending on how many are eating and how many are serving. It takes considerable practice to know what rules to apply when, not to mention how to keep the sleeves of your robe from getting in the way as you serve. It would be one thing if there was someone kind to teach you, but you can't hope for this in a monastery. The norm is that you learn the hard way, making mistakes and getting yelled at as you go.

How I Discovered Monastic Practice in a Bowl of Cold Noodles

The Cold Noodles on Chū-chan's Menu

Once, when I was in the role of master's attendant, I accompanied my teacher, Sōchū, to Tokyo. Midday came, and I was just beginning to wonder what we'd do about lunch when he suggested we go and find somewhere to eat together.

Great! I thought. A rare chance to eat out in the world! Food in the monastery is meagre. There's surely nothing wrong with a bit of luxury now and then. Hmm, what will I have? Maybe some sushi? Or how about Chinese noodles? Oh, I'd love some tempura. In monk's robes it wouldn't do to go eating meat, of course . . .

So my mind ran wildly on.

'Ah, let's go in here,' he said, and stepped into a little place called Chū-chan's Restaurant.

There were other places around, grills and eateries of various sorts, so why did he make a point of choosing this pokey little place? I thought. Was it because of the connection with his own name?

To be honest, I was pretty disheartened. Big expectations create big disappointments, and I felt very glum. The name of the restaurant suggested that it wouldn't have much going for it, and when we went in and saw the menu it was just as I'd thought.

The menu was only one page long, so it took no time to run my eye over the offerings. Thick and thin noodles, curry rice and various rice dishes. On the wall was a little blackboard with the words 'Today's special: boiled mackerel'.

'I'll have the cold noodles,' said Sōchū with barely a glance at the menu.

'Right, I'll have the rice omelette.'

Before long our two dishes arrived.

'Mm, these noodles look good,' said Sōchū, and he started to eat them. But after a moment he declared, 'No, they're no good after all.'

Chū-chan's Food

Shichimi spice bottle, spices stuck to the bottom

Cheap bowl

Thin spongy noodles

Noodles slopped in off-centre

Dried-out chopped spring onion

Chopsticks

'Chū-chan is proud of his food'

Dashi sauce tasting of MSG

Tray with a broken corner

He put down his chopsticks, and then he sat there serenely gazing at my omelette.

'Would you like to swap?' I said tentatively.

He nodded vigorously and beamed like a little kid.

And so I ended up eating the tasteless cold noodles.

There was still some time before our appointment, so he suggested dropping in somewhere for some tea. We went into a coffee shop next to Chū-chan's Restaurant.

I ordered coffee, and some sandwiches to get rid of the taste of the noodles.

Sōchū examined the menu. 'Look, they have noodles here too,' he said, and happily ordered another serving of cold noodles. He just loved those noodles!

'I'll just go to the toilet,' he announced, and off he went.

The next moment there was a voice from the back door. 'Hi, Chū-chan from next door here with your cold noodles.'

Chū-chan's noodles? I panicked. Surely not! This must be some kind of joke. I began to sweat. But sure enough, the cold noodles were placed on our table as if this was all perfectly normal.

It's weird for a coffee shop to offer cold noodles so there must have been something else going on here – some family relationship between the two establishments, perhaps.

I'd had to eat that first horrible cold noodle dish as a result of opening my big mouth, but I was damned if I was going to have to eat the second.

As soon as Sōchū came back, I announced that the noodles this time were apparently specially hand-made.

'Aha, is that so?' He set about slurping them down.

'Delicious!' he declared. 'So much better than Chū-chan's were!'

I seem to remember hearing a similar story in a traditional comic monologue once, but my story is actually true. And there is an important second chapter to it.

Your Practice Continues Here Too

It's the custom in the monastery to eat meals in silence, but on this occasion for some reason Sōchū was in the mood to chat.

'You know, it's best to enjoy noodles straight without adding the usual spring onion, sesame seeds, seaweed and so on. And *shichimi* spice is particularly terrible. The fact is, you have to get rid of all the unnecessary stuff to really appreciate the essential taste. Yes, noodles are best when they're just noodles. It all comes down to the water. Just take a sip of the water they put out for you when you enter a restaurant and you'll know what sort of cooking you're in for . . .'

I was lost in my own thoughts, and wasn't paying much attention to what he said, but thinking over his words later I realized that he must have actually known perfectly well that his second bowl of noodles was as bad as the first.

Why did he order that second bowl?

The answer to this question was provided that evening.

It was a little after eight when we got back to the monastery after Sōchū's business in the outside world was done.

I got out of the taxi at the temple gate and set off quickly, carrying his bag. From the gate you have to climb a fairly long stone staircase to get to the monastery. My mind was full of thoughts of what was ahead – first Sōchū must change out of his visiting clothes, then I needed to check telephone and mail messages, put his clothes away ... I'd climbed the stairs and was just about to go in when I heard his footsteps behind me suddenly come to a halt.

I turned. He was looking steadily at me.

'Your practice continues here too, you know,' he said.

I was silent, not really understanding.

'Hey, snap out of it! Get my bath ready,' he said sharply.

What on earth was he trying to tell me? I mean, I knew perfectly well that my practice continued inside the monastery.

The reason he said this, I now think, was to tell me that the outside world beyond the monastery doors was also a place where one's practice continues. He was teaching me that the day in Tokyo and our rides to and from it had been part of Zen practice.

Tokyo ...

I looked back over my behaviour in Tokyo that day.

Straight off the train at Tokyo Station, my eye had been caught by a crowd of young schoolgirls. In the world of the monastery it's rare to catch a glimpse of a girl, and every one of them looked beautiful to me. Next, my attention was snared by the restaurants. All those menus in the windows looked so delicious that my heart leapt with pleasure like a child's. Clearly, Sōchū had detected all this from my behaviour and where my eyes wandered.

Similarly with Chū-chan's Restaurant and the next-door coffee shop. *So what's this attendant of mine going to order? If he's continuing his monastic practice, he should order the sort of food he'd eat there.* These were no doubt the thoughts that were going through his head.

I'd simply thought that he ordered noodles because he loved them, but such was not the case. Sōchū ordered noodles because wherever he was was a place of Zen practice for him.

Then he must have swapped his noodles for my rice omelette to see how I ate the noodles. I'd added a heap of *shichimi* spice to try to improve the taste, though in the monastery it's a basic rule to add no spices to food. This is because they leave the mouth stimulated, getting in the way of the concentration required for meditation. This was what lay behind that little lecture I received in the coffee shop about the right way to eat noodles.

Looking back over all this made me blush with shame. What a sorry figure I'd cut! He must have watched with a private bitter smile as I forgot all about being a monk and let myself get high on the heady atmosphere of Tokyo. Well, it was a rare event so he probably forgave me, I decided. Those words of his as I entered the monastery again – *Your practice continues here too, you know* – seemed to me the kind of passing scolding that a parent would feel obliged to give.

Both making food and eating it are part of one's practice. If your mind becomes distracted, practice is no longer practice. And practice is not just something that happens in a monastic setting – it happens wherever you are.

That was truly a day for me to remember, the day when I understood Zen practice through a bowl of cold noodles.

4

A Brief History of Zen

Before Zen Came to Japan

The Birth of Buddhism

Here I'd like to give you a very simple history of Zen, and of the Rinzai sect in particular. This will require a bit of explanation, so if you get bored please feel free to skip ahead.

Let me start with the man behind Zen, the Buddha himself. I suggest you consult the illustrative map of the Buddha's life (on page 65) from time to time as you read.

The man known as the Buddha, whose name was Shakyamuni, first saw the world on 8 April 463 BC, at the foot of the Himalayan mountains in a place called Lumbini (in present-day Nepal).

There are actually a number of theories about his exact dates.

1. Around 624–544 BC.
2. Around 566–486 BC.
3. Around 463–383 BC.

Most Buddhist scholars in Japan prefer either 2 or 3 above.

Buddhist literature names his father as Suddhodana and his mother as Maya. His father was king of the kingdom of Shakya – although Shakya was really too small to deserve the name 'kingdom', and he was probably more like a clan chief. 'Shakya' in the name Shakyamuni is thus the name of his tribe. Shakyamuni means the Holy One of the Shaka tribe. The term 'Buddha' that's often used to refer to him means 'Enlightened One'; one whose eyes are opened to the Truth.

His father and mother weren't blessed with offspring, and both they and their people greeted the birth of the long-awaited prince with delight. But an unexpected misfortune awaited him. Seven days after he was born his mother died, perhaps from postnatal complications.

As a child, he went by the name Guatama Siddhartha. Siddhartha means 'one who achieves his goal'. Guatama, the family name of the Shaka tribe, means 'sacred cow'. It's a name you'd expect to find in a place like India where cattle are revered.

Because his early name was Siddhartha I should really refer to him as Prince Siddhartha to begin with, but since it's confusing to keep changing names I'll keep to the name Shakyamuni.

Shakyamuni grew up lacking nothing in life. He married a beautiful girl and had a beautiful son, and on the face of it his life seemed enviable in every way. But at the age of twenty-nine he experienced a great spiritual awakening, and he left his home and became a monk.

This is the story that has come down to us about his spiritual awakening.

Four times Shakyamuni went out of the palace gate, and each time he was confronted by a different sight. First he saw an old person, next he saw a sick person, next he saw a corpse. Finally, it was a renunciate that met his eyes, one who has turned his back on the world to follow a spiritual path. In this way, he was confronted with the fundamental realities of existence – old age, illness, death, and the possibility of spiritual awakening.

The fundamental suffering of worldly existence – the transience of life, and its futility – struck him deeply. Seeking a solution, he followed the way of the renunciate and renounced the world.

His father sought to stop him, and in his anxiety set five guards to prevent his son from fulfilling his wish. These five men later followed Shakyamuni into the path of renunciation.

Shakyamuni first went to two holy men to seek answers, but nothing they said satisfied him. Eventually, he chose to dedicate himself to fierce austerities such as fasting in his pursuit of an answer. And after six years of a life of austerity, he understood: this was foolish. Extreme austerity was not the way to attain enlightenment.

Map of the Buddha's Life

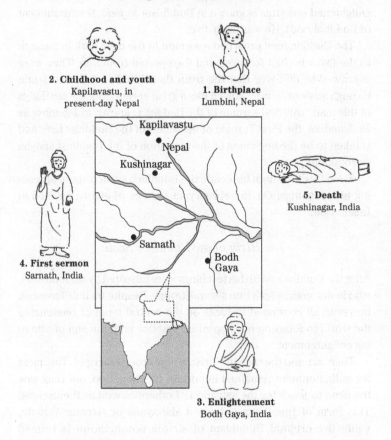

2. Childhood and youth
Kapilavastu, in
present-day Nepal

1. Birthplace
Lumbini, Nepal

Kapilavastu

Nepal

Kushinagar

Sarnath

Bodh
Gaya

5. Death
Kushinagar, India

4. First sermon
Sarnath, India

3. Enlightenment
Bodh Gaya, India

He bathed his body in the Niranjana River, in what is now northern India, and was nursed back to health with the help of a village maiden named Sujata who gave him milk gruel.

The five men who had followed him, however, were disappointed that he had abandoned austerity, and they parted ways with him.

Shakyamuni now began to meditate beneath a bo tree in Bodh Gaya. Having entered a state of deep meditation, early on the morning of 8 December he attained enlightenment and became a buddha or enlightened one (this is known in Buddhism as *jōdō*, the Attainment of Buddhahood). He was thirty-five.

The Buddha now preached a sermon in the deer park in Sarnath to the five who had followed and then parted from him. They were overawed to discover that the truth that they had failed to attain through austerities now flowed like a great spring from the teachings of this man. This first sermon of the Buddha is known in Japanese as *shotenbōrin*, the First Turning of the Wheel of the Buddhist Law, and is taken to be the beginning of the formation of the Buddhist sangha or community.

From this time until his death, the Buddha travelled about spreading his teachings. On 15 February, at the age of eighty, he died in Kushinagar.

The Birth of the Buddhist Sects

After the Buddha's death his teachings were inherited by his followers, who in due course split into several groups. Despite their differences, however, all continued to focus on the central tenet of renouncing the world to focus on one's spiritual practice with the aim of attaining enlightenment.

Then, around the time of Christ, a new group emerged. The quest for enlightenment remained important for them, too, but they saw the need to work for the salvation of others as well as themselves. This form of Buddhism is termed Mahayana or Greater Vehicle, while the original Buddhism of simple renunciation is termed Hinayana or Lesser Vehicle. The two can be seen as reformists and conservatives.

Hinayana Buddhism spread to south-east Asian countries such as Sri Lanka, Myanmar, Thailand, Cambodia and Laos. Mahayana went north, to Tibet, China, Korea and Japan.

Buddhism reached Japan via China and Korea in around the sixth century. Japan's great early ruler, Shōtoku Taishi (574–622), was instrumental in encouraging Buddhism to take root in Japan. He drew up laws based on Buddhist teaching, and studied and annotated various Buddhist sutras or sacred texts.

Shōtoku Taishi founded the great early temple of Shintennōji (in present-day Osaka), which offered shelter to the ill and the destitute. He also left a wonderful Buddhist legacy with the construction of Nara temples like the great Hōryūji and Chūgūji, and he sent envoys to China to directly import more Buddhist teaching.

I've gone into quite a lot of detail to bring the story this far, but I'll now move more quickly.

Up until around the eighth century, Buddhism in Japan remained an imported teaching and was limited to scholarly study, but in that century (the Nara period) Japanese Buddhism split into six sects. Many monks studied in two sects simultaneously, however, and temples were generally not divided into sects. Buddhism in Japan at this time was essentially a magical religion devoted to rituals for protecting the nation and ensuring good harvests.

Japanese Buddhism took roughly its present form in the early Heian period with the two founders Saichō (767–822) and Kūkai (774–835), who established the Tendai and Shingon sects respectively. From this point on, Buddhism began to shift from being a purely scholarly religion to becoming a religion of faith.

Then about 400 years later, there was a sudden rush of new sects. Chief among them were the Jōdo or Pure Land sect, the Ji sect, and the two schools of Zen (Rinzai and Sōtō), followed by the Nichiren sect.

Behind this sudden surge of new Buddhist sects was a historical shift from the aristocrat-centred world of the Heian period to the dominance of military families (samurai) that came to power with the Kamakura period. This was accompanied by huge social upheaval and warfare. People felt lost and anxious, and their fears found expression in the Buddhist concept of the Latter Days.

According to the Buddhist view of history, the strength of Buddhism will wane as the centuries pass. In the first age, teaching, practice and enlightenment occur harmoniously. In the following age, there are still

History of Japanese Buddhist Sects and Founders
from 538 (or 552) arrival of Buddhism

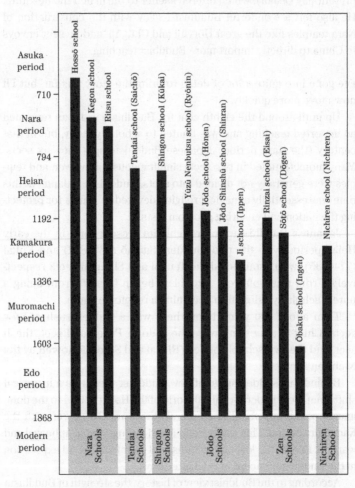

Characteristics of the 13 Main Japanese Buddhist Sects

Sect name	Founder	When established	Central texts	Focus of worship	Lineage
Hossō		Asuka	Kegon-ron	Shaka Nyorai	
Kegon	Saichō	Nara	Kegon Sutra	Bibashana	Nara Buddhism
Ritsu		Nara	Shibunritsuzō	Bibashana	
Tendai	Kūkai	Heian	Lotus Sutra, Dainichi Sutra, Amida Sutra	Shaka Nyorai	Tendai
Shingon	Ryōnin	Heian	Dainich Sutra, Kongōchō Sutra	Dainichi	Shingon
Yūzū Nenbutsu	Hōnen	Heian	Kegon Sutra, Lotus Sutra, Muryōju Sutra	Amida	
Jōdo	Shinran	Heian	Muryōju Sutra, Kanmurryō Sutra, Amida Sutra	Amida	Jōdo
Jōdo Shin	Ippen	Kamakura	(not based on written word)	Amida	
Ji	Eisai	Kamakura	(not based on written word)	Amida	
Rinzai	Dōgen	Kamakura	(not based on written word)	Shaka Nyorai	
Sōtō	Ingen	Kamakura	Lotus Sutra	Shaka Nyorai	Zen
Ōbaku	Nichiren	Edo	?	Shaka Nyorai	
Nichiren	?	Kamakura	?	Shaka Nyorai	Nichiren

people who practise but none who are enlightened. In the final or Latter age, no teachers remain. One theory holds that each age lasts 500 years, another says each lasts 1,000 years. In Japan, the year 1052 was held to mark the beginning of the Latter Days. The sense of crisis that this created brought forth a series of founders of new forms of Buddhism.

One set of beliefs held that in these degenerate Latter Days it was not possible for an individual to gain enlightenment on his or her own, and people should instead place their faith in Amida Buddha who would bring them to the Pure Land paradise. This kind of Buddhism is called *tariki* (other-power or salvation from without), and it is exemplified by the various Jōdo or Pure Land sects.

Others held that in these Latter Days it was instead imperative to return to the fundamental teachings of Buddhism, to the true law. This kind of Buddhism is called *jiriki* (self-power or salvation through one's own efforts), and it is exemplified by Zen Buddhism.

I have briefly explained the history of Japanese Buddhism up to the emergence of Zen. Next I want to focus on the Rinzai sect of Zen in more detail.

Before I leave the general story, page 69 brings Japanese Buddhism into the present with a table laying out the thirteen basic sects and schools. In it I try to give a quick summary of the characteristics of each, although this can be difficult. In the category 'focus of worship' I give the name of the particular buddha or bodhisattva that the sect takes as its principle image for worship, although in fact this can vary.

The History and Teachings of the Rinzai Zen School

A School without a Founder

The special characteristics of the Rinzai school can probably be summed up in the following five points:

1. Its teachings go back to the fundamental teachings of the Buddha.
2. They have branched off into various forms.
3. It was Eisai who brought the Rinzai teachings to Japan in 1191, but his direct lineage has since died out.
4. The Rinzai teachings in their present form are based on the teachings of the eighteenth-century Japanese monk Hakuin.
5. The essential Rinzai teachings cannot be communicated in words.

Point 1 is probably self-evident, really. The teachings of the Buddha himself form the basis of every sect of Buddhism, after all. But for Zen, the point is that the Buddha attained enlightenment through meditation – though I should point out that meditation was not his own invention, but had existed in India since antiquity.

I should also make clear that the Zen sect did not come into existence directly after the Buddha's enlightenment. Bodhidharma founded Zen – or Ch'an, as it is called in China – by bringing the Buddhist teaching from India to China. This is believed to have happened around AD 520. This teaching was then passed down from one teacher to the next.

The founder of the Rinzai school in China was a monk called Rinzai Gigen (? –867). The other main Zen school, Sōtō, was founded by Tōzan Ryōkai (807–69). They were both active around the same time but were of different Buddhist lineages.

The Rinzai school then split into the Ōryū and Yōgi schools. Eisai, the founder of Japanese Rinzai who twice went to China to bring back the Rinzai teachings, was affiliated with the Ōryū line. He had numerous followers, some of whom went back to China after his death to receive further instruction.

Among them was a monk called Dōgen. On his return, he spent some time in the Kyoto temple of Kenninji that Eisai had founded, then decided to found his own separate school. If Dōgen had stayed in the school established by Eisai, Japanese Zen would no doubt have taken a different course.

The Lineage of the Zen Sect

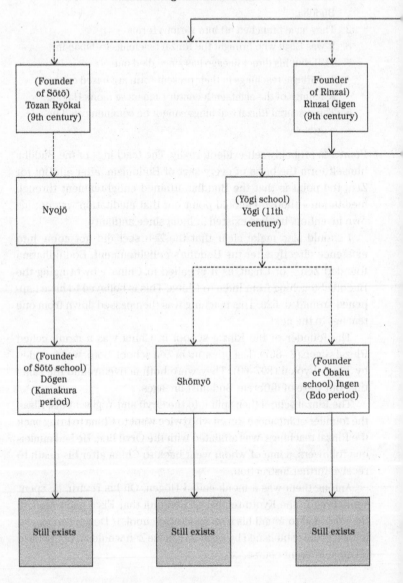

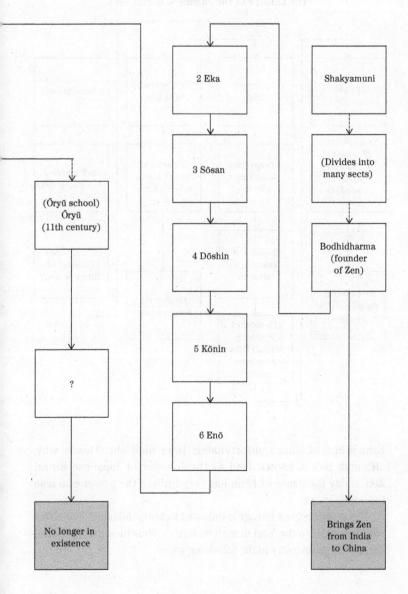

The Lineage of the Japanese Rinzai Sect

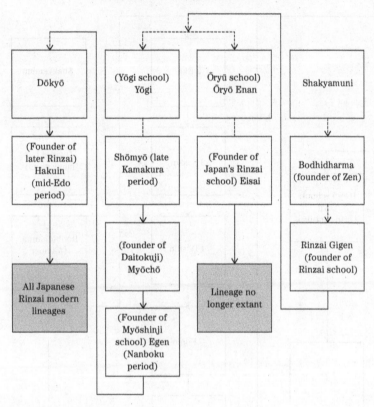

Eisai's line of Rinzai unfortunately later died out. This is why, although he's acknowledged as the founder of Japanese Rinzai Zen, today the figure of Eisai has very little of the power of a true founder.

The person whose lineage is followed today is Hakuin (1685–1768), who belonged to the Yōgi branch of Rinzai. Thus modern-day Rinzai Zen traces its ancestry in the following way:

Buddha → Bodhidharma → Daiō → Daitō (founder of Daitokuji
Temple) → Kanzan (founder of Myōshinji Temple) → Hakuin

Eisai is not included in this line. Instead we have Daiō, who in the
thirteenth century went to China and brought back teachings in the
Yōgi line, which he passed on to Daitō and so on eventually to Hakuin.

Hakuin inherited these teachings and added his own system of
kōan, thereby structuring Rinzai Zen into its Japanese form. When
we consider that it's really his form of Zen that the Rinzai school
has inherited today, perhaps in fact the school should be called
Hakuin Zen.

Besides the Rinzai and Sōtō schools, Japan also has the smaller
Ōbaku school, founded by the Chinese monk Ingen (1592–1673).
This is the youngest of the thirteen Zen schools, but considering that
Hakuin was active about 100 years after this it could be said that the
modern form of Rinzai is in fact the youngest.

Nevertheless, Hakuin is not the same kind of important founder
figure that the other sects have. He is not really revered in the way
the other sects revere their founders. Zen seems to stand out from
other sects in honouring the teachings themselves rather than the
founder.

The image in the altar in Zen temples is that of Shakyamuni Buddha,
although other images can also be present. There are also no fixed
sacred texts as there are in other sects.

Teaching That Can't
be Communicated in Words

Let me tell you a story that exemplifies Zen teaching. This story is in
fact one of the Rinzai school's *kōans* and is found in the *Mumonkan*.

One day, the Buddha was to preach a sermon on Vulture Peak, a
place well-known as the site of his sermons.

He arrived at his seat and his many followers waited expect-
antly for him to begin.

Now came the sound of bird calls as a crowd of little birds arrived. Rabbits, squirrels, deer – many animals were also gathering to hear him. Still the Buddha sat there, speaking not a word.

'What can be the matter?'

'Perhaps he's feeling ill?'

'No, perhaps he's wondering what to say to us?'

His followers murmured among themselves in consternation.

Then the Buddha raised a flower he was holding and lightly twirled it.

'Ah!' exclaimed Kashō, one of his disciples, and smiled.

The Buddha observed this, and his gaze met Kashō's. Then the Buddha finally spoke.

'I have just shown Kashō the invisible realm of enlightenment,' he said.

In the original text, the Buddha's words are:

I have the eye treasury of right Dharma, the subtle mind of nirvana, the true form of no-form, and the flawless gate of the teaching. It is not established upon words and phrases. It is a special transmission outside tradition. I now entrust this to Kashō.*

'The eye treasury of right Dharma' means the correct teaching. The eye treasury is the eyes to see all things. The treasury is the place where all things are stored. Essentially, this means 'the power to apply the teachings of the buddhas'. In other words, it is the realm of enlightenment.

'The subtle mind of nirvana', 'the true form of no-form', and 'the flawless gate of the teaching' all refer to the same thing – enlightenment.

Any teaching conveyed by words is in danger of being misunderstood. Even if your intention is to speak of A and B, listeners will often put a different interpretation on what you say. The Buddha wanted only to use the right means of giving his teachings. This is where the true power of Buddhism lies, it seems to me.

* In the translation of Robert Aitken, *The Gateless Barrier: The We-Men Kuan (Momonkan)*, North Point Press, 1995; p. 46.

This story may lack historical truth, but I think it beautifully expresses the special quality of Zen teachings.

So what happens when this story is given as a Zen *kōan* for meditation? Just like the *kōans* I presented in Chapter 1, the story itself is the question. The Buddha's words simply embody that question. I know I've said this many times now, but it's worth repeating.

5

The Heart Sutra and
the World of '*Kū*'

Warm-up: The Heart Sutra

The Relationship between the
Heart Sutra and Zen

The aim of Zen practice is to become one with the enlightened state attained by the Buddha through meditation. As I explained in the last chapter, Zen teaches that the actual substance of this enlightenment is not something that words can communicate.

This can also be said of the two key words in Zen, *mu* and *kū*.

I've already talked about *mu* in Chapter 1, in relation to the *kōan* about Chao-chou's Dog. It's the first thing you discover when you use *kōans* in Zen meditation.

As for *kū*, it's best known from the famous words of the Heart Sutra – '*shiki soku ze kū, kū soku ze shiki*', which can be translated as 'form is emptiness (*kū*), emptiness is form'. I think that in Zen terms you could say that *kū* and *mu* are more or less the same thing as what is termed enlightenment. By arriving at one, you arrive at the others.

So let's look a bit more closely at this *kū*. I'd like to tell you some of my thoughts about *kū* by explaining a bit about the Heart Sutra. First, though, let me just quickly fill you in about the sutras used in the Rinzai school of Zen.

Many Buddhist sects have specific sutras that are central to their teaching and worship – the Pure Land Sutras (Jōdokyō) in the Jōdo sects, the Lotus Sutra (Hokekyō) in the Nichiren sect and so on. But this is not the case with the Zen sects.

That doesn't mean we don't use sutras – we do. A list of the sutras commonly chanted in the Rinzai school would include:

1. Very short sutras such as Kaikyōge or Sangemon.
2. Relatively short sutras such as Segaki and the Heart Sutra (Hannya shingyō).
3. Somewhat longer sutras (for example, the Lotus Sutra).
4. Long sutras (for example, Kongōkyō).

In a Buddhist service there's a fixed order to the sutras we chant – Heart Sutra, Shōsaikyō, Daihikyō, Lotus Sutra, Butchō Sonchō Darani – though there are some variations between temples and between regions. But the ones that are most often chanted would be the Heart Sutra, Daihikyō and Butchō Sonchō Darani.

The Heart Sutra is commonly used in many sects, but it can be said of Zen sects in general that this sutra is the embodiment of Zen doctrine.

The fact is, the Heart Sutra is very popular in Japan – indeed, it's the most popular of the sutras. For example, it constitutes about 80 per cent of the sutras that appear in TV dramas and anime films. The rest are either the Fudō mantra or bits of other popular sutras such as the Lotus Sutra.

Why is the Heart Sutra so popular?

1. It's used in many Buddhist sects.
2. It's short enough to be easily memorized.
3. Its contents are profound.

But it's no easy matter to actually translate this sutra into everyday language and explain its meaning. There are some very challenging problems involved.

1. If you translate faithfully from the original, it doesn't make much sense.
2. There are quite a few words in it that aren't easy to understand.
3. In fact, the theme of the sutra itself is difficult to understand.

The Structure of the Heart Sutra

What is *kū*?

Kannon Bodhisattva understood *kū* through the Heart Sutra

There is no coming into being, and no extinction of being

Kannon Bodhisattva was released from all suffering through understanding *kū*

There is no Buddhist teaching

This world is *kū*

Final mantra

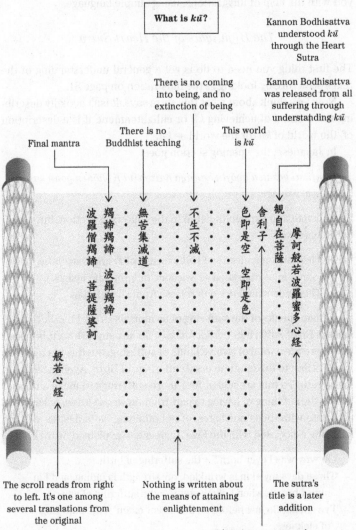

羯諦羯諦　　波羅羯諦　波羅僧羯諦　菩提薩婆訶

無苦集滅道

不生不滅

色即是空　空即是色

舍利子

観自在菩薩

摩訶般若波羅蜜多心経

般若心経

The scroll reads from right to left. It's one among several translations from the original

Nothing is written about the means of attaining enlightenment

It's written as a speech directed to Sariputra

The sutra's title is a later addition

However, I'll try to make some sense of it by reading it through with you with the help of illustrations, using simple language.

The Highlights of the Heart Sutra

The first thing you need to do is get a general understanding of the text's structure by looking at the illustration on page 81.

Now let's think about what this sutra says. It isn't actually describing the method of achieving *kū* or enlightenment, it is a description of 'the world of *kū*' or the world as *kū*.

In Japanese, the opening section goes:

Kanjizai bosatsu gyōjin hannya haramita ji shōken goun kaikū doissai kuyaku

I'll translate and explain in detail in the following section, but essentially this says:

1. The Kannon understood *kū* by means of *Prajna paramita* (sometimes translated as 'wisdom' or 'profound insight').
2. This understanding led to release from all suffering.

Buddhism speaks of the suffering of us mortals as the Four Sufferings and the Eight Sufferings (*shiku hakku*). Some people think this means that there are a total of twelve kinds of suffering, but this is a mistake. It refers first to the four universal sufferings of Birth, Ageing, Sickness and Death. To this are added four more sufferings to make a total of eight – the suffering of having to part from those one loves, of having to associate with those one hates, of not attaining one's desires, and the suffering associated with the Five Aggregates (explained below).

'Oh why was I ever born?' = the suffering of birth.
'These days my skin is wrinkled, my strength is fading, and I'm out of breath when I climb stairs' = the suffering of age.
'I've caught flu just before an important exam' = the suffering of sickness.
'I don't want to die!' = the suffering of death.

'You said you'd love me for ever and now you've changed
   your mind!' = the suffering of having to part from those one
   loves.
'Work would be so much better if it weren't for that boss I have' =
   the suffering of having to associate with those one hates.
'Why can't I manage to get married?' = the suffering of not attaining one's desires.
'I just feel so lonely and alone in the world' = the suffering associated with the Five Aggregates.

The suffering of birth is also believed by some to mean the suffering
of the child as it passes through the birth canal, in which case it would
go something like this:

'It's dark . . . it's tight . . . ooh, it hurts . . . this is horrible' = the
   suffering of birth.

An understanding of $k\bar{u}$ liberates you from these sufferings.

So what is this liberating thing we call $k\bar{u}$? Let's read the words of
the sutra more closely.

The Universe of the Heart Sutra

All is Kū

The very first words are the title – *maka hannya haramita*. These
words are a Japanese transliteration of the ancient Indian language
of Sanskrit, the language that the sutra was first written in. A closer
transcription of the original Sanskrit words would be *maha prajna
paramita*, which translated means roughly 'great', 'wisdom' and
'attains the other side' (that is, the realm of enlightenment).

Like most others, this sutra was first translated into Chinese and later
brought over to Japan. In Chinese, the name 'Heart Sutra' means 'central sutra', which is thought to express the idea that this sutra contains
the essence of all the 600 volumes of the great *Prajna paramita Sutra*.

To summarize, then, the full name of this sutra means 'the central sutra of the great wisdom of enlightenment'.

The man who first translated this sutra from Sanskrit into Chinese was Xuanzang (602–64). This famous monk travelled to India and collected a great many sutras, which he then translated to take back to China. He might also be familiar to you in the guise of Tripitaka in the wonderful Chinese story *The Journey to the West*, sometimes known as *Monkey*.

Now let's return to the opening words of the sutra:

Kanjizai bosatsu gyōjin hannya haramita ji shōken goun kaikū doissai kuyaku.

This can be roughly translated as:

Through the deep practice of *Prajna paramita*, Kannon Bodhisattva perceived that all the Five Aggregates were *kū* (empty), and was liberated from all suffering.

Prajna paramita is the last in the list of the six paths or disciplines leading to enlightenment (the Six *Paramitas*) – generous giving, precepts, fortitude, devotion, meditation and wisdom. It means the strength or wisdom to see and act correctly.

This is the most important of the six paths. The other five are considered preparation for its attainment, but at the same time this wisdom is necessary for the correct performance of the other five paths. The word 'deep' here means that he devoted himself single-mindedly, tirelessly and over a long period.

So by means of this *Prajna paramita* (the power to perceive and act correctly), the bodhisattva was able to perceive that the 'Five Aggregates' are *kū*.

The Five Aggregates is a Buddhist term essentially meaning the material world (referred to as 'forms') plus the four mental activities – those of the five senses, perception, the impulse to action, and consciousness. Early Indian philosophers held that our world is constructed from these five things. (See the illustration 'This World is Entirely *Kū*' on page 87).

The Six Practices Leading to Understanding Kū

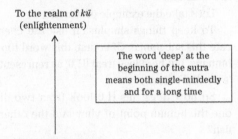

To the realm of *kū*
(enlightenment)

The word 'deep' at the beginning of the sutra means both single-mindedly and for a long time

The Six *Paramitas*

Generosity	Precepts	Fortitude	Devotion	Meditation	Wisdom
Be generous to others	Keep the rules	Be firm and determined	Devote yourself to your practice	Purify your mind	Perceive and act correctly

The realm of suffering and delusion

According to one Buddhist dictionary's definition, the word *kū* expresses the idea that 'the things that exist have no essential substance, being or self.' It's a difficult idea, I agree.

So what manner of thing are these Five Aggregates that are said to be empty or '*kū*'? We can summarize by saying this term refers to this world of ours. The real problem is the word '*kū*'. It's extremely difficult to try to state the meaning of the statement 'the Five Aggregates are *kū*' in straightforward, everyday language, but it might go something like this: 'Everything in this world is essentially empty. All these things that you name and perceive as real are fundamentally non-existent.'

Let's take the example of water.

To keep things simple, I'll use the chemical term H_2O to indicate this substance. Of course this word too has been created by us humans, but here let's treat 'H_2O' as representing the fact of water, its 'essential nature'.

So how does this H_2O look from two different points of view, one the human point of view and the other the point of view of a fish?

Humans see it as water, fish see it as home.

Of course we can't borrow the eyes of a fish so this is just a hypothesis. But my point is, 'water' is simply the word or concept we use to refer to the substance H_2O, and in fact this 'water' doesn't exist in and of itself. It just expresses our experience of H_2O, not its essential nature.

When we experience the physical world, we perceive it through the words or names we use for it. As we do this, we're actually calling to mind the concepts that we've already learned to associate with those words, and at the same time we're feeling something. But none of these things actually exist except in our own minds.

The substance H_2O existed before humans appeared on earth. Then we came along and applied the word 'water' to it. We learned various things about this 'water', and put them together to make our understanding of what 'water' is.

Some of these – such as the fact that water quenches our thirst, that it's necessary for life, or that it's precious – provoke feelings in us. But whatever name we give it, however we look at it, H_2O simply exists as H_2O. Essentially, it's not the thing that we've created through our thoughts and feelings about it. That 'water' doesn't really exist in its own right, independent of our thoughts and feelings.

So, the text continues, once you understand that the Five Aggregates, this world we experience, are essentially empty or *kū*, you are freed from all suffering (meaning the Four Sufferings and the Eight Sufferings described above).

This World is Entirely *Kū*

The Five Aggregates All the things in the world	色	物質	Form	Material world (physical world as the object of our perception)
	受	感覚	Sensations	Mental world (the actions of the mind)
	想	思い	Perceptions	
	行	意志	Volitions	
	識	認識	Consciousness	

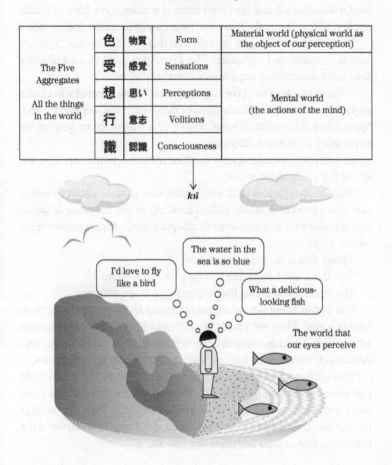

kū

The water in the sea is so blue

I'd love to fly like a bird

What a delicious-looking fish

The world that our eyes perceive

Oh Sariputra, form is not other than emptiness, emptiness is not other than form. Form is emptiness, emptiness is form. This is also true of sensation, perception, volition and consciousness.

87

Sariputra was one of the Buddha's ten great disciples. He was said to be the wisest of all, and the Heart Sutra is written in the form of words spoken to him. Actually, however, its message is aimed at everyone.

In the first sentence, we are told that this world is *kū*, and then this idea is re-stated and expanded. The Five Aggregates (forms plus the four mental activities, explained earlier) are all *kū*.

As an example of the Five Aggregates being *kū*, think of what I said earlier about H_2O being a completely different thing, depending on a human or a fish's point of view. 'Water' (the substance or form as we experience it) is essentially *kū*.

In order to understand how the four mental activities are also *kū*, let's think again about water.

Imagine two glasses of filtered water. One glass is tasted by someone who's used to drinking chlorinated tap water, the other is tasted by someone who has only ever drunk pure bottled spring water from Mount Fuji.

'Mmm, this is delicious,' says one.

'You think so? I don't like it much,' says the other.

The water is the same, the responses to it are different.

The fact is, there is no such substance as 'delicious water' or 'bad-tasting water'. They are simply the different judgements of the people who taste it. And these judgements can't be relied on either. If you were desperately thirsty, even the bad-tasting water would taste delicious.

There are any number of examples like this. The person you adored last year now turns you right off. We hear such stories all the time, don't we? And it can just as easily go the other way. People's feelings are incredibly changeable. So it's actually quite easy to understand the statement that mental activities are also *kū*.

> Sariputra, all dharmas are in their nature emptiness, neither born nor extinguished, neither foul nor pure, neither increasing nor decreasing.

The phrase 'all dharmas' (*shohō*) refers to the world composed by the Five Aggregates. You could translate it as 'all phenomena' or 'all existences'. These include not just physical things but also abstract mental activities such as concepts and feelings.

The statement 'neither born nor extinguished' is sometimes explained in terms of water, which can be boiled and turned into steam but still exists even though its form is altered. But I don't think such examples need to be spelled out. This world is *kū* – that's why its phenomena have no birth or death, aren't dirty or clean, neither increase nor decrease. It's just that we have various judgements, ideas and ways of thinking about them and distinguishing them.

> For this reason, in *kū* there are no form, no feeling, perception, volition, consciousness. No eyes, ears, nose, tongue, body or mind. No sight, sound, scent, taste, touch or phenomena. No world of seeing, through to no world of consciousness.

These statements use the Buddhist concepts of the Five Aggregates (form, sensation, perception, volition, consciousness), plus the Eighteen Realms – these consist of the Six Sense Organs, the Six Sense Objects and the Six Consciousnesses.

The Six Sense Organs (*rokkon*) are the body's six means of directly perceiving the world.

The Six Sense Objects (*rokkyō*) are the six kinds of phenomena perceived by the sense organs.

The Six Consciousnesses (*rokushiki*) are the various reactions between these sense organs and sense objects. The sutra does not list all the Six Consciousnesses, just abbreviates them to the first and last.

The relationship between these Eighteen Realms can be explained with the example of your eyes. Because you have the sense organs called eyes, you perceive H_2O in the visual realm of sense objects, and your visual consciousness interprets this as water. If you then think 'I'm thirsty' and drink it, your judgements about its taste come into play.

But the Heart Sutra says that all these – the Five Aggregates and the Eighteen Realms – are nothing (*mu*). The sutra goes on:

> No ignorance, also no extinction of ignorance; no ageing or death, also no extinction of ageing and death. No suffering, no cause of suffering, no cessation, no path; no wisdom, no attainment.

To summarize, this passage says that in *kū* neither the Twelve Links of Interdependent Arising nor the Four Noble Truths nor the realm of enlightenment exist.

To explain in order: the first sentence provides an abbreviated list of the Twelve Links of Interdependent Arising, the Buddhist teaching about the various forms of human suffering and the means of release from them.

The relationship between these is:

> Ignorance → power of formation → act of cognition → names and shapes → the six sense organs → contact → feeling → love → attachment → existence → birth → ageing and death

In other words, ignorance is the cause of all suffering, and if ignorance is extinguished then human suffering will also be extinguished.

'No suffering, no cause of suffering, no cessation, no path' refers to what's called the Four Noble Truths. To put it simply, this doctrine explains how human suffering can be extinguished.

> Suffering: Correctly analyse the present situation . . . Recognize the fact of human suffering.
>
> Cause of Suffering: Consider the cause of suffering . . . Recognize the fact that suffering is caused by desire and attachment.
>
> Cessation: Consider how to solve this problem . . . Relinquish desire and attachment.
>
> Path: The practical method and practice that achieves this . . . Following the teachings of the Buddha.

Finally, 'no wisdom, no attainment'. Wisdom is the understanding of the Buddhist teachings. Attainment is the attainment of enlightenment.

Here the Heart Sutra is essentially saying that in the realm of *kū* even the Buddhist teachings don't exist.

Well then, you might think, why should I try to learn and practise these teachings? But in fact it's natural that the Buddhist teachings don't exist in this *kū* realm where there are no concepts, feelings or abstract phenomena at all.

> Having no attainment, Bodhisattvas rely on *Prajna paramita* and therefore have no attachment in their heart, and having no attachment they therefore have no fear, and having gone utterly beyond all wrong perceptions they realize complete Nirvana.

This is essentially re-stating the content of the very first passage in the Heart Sutra. To sum up the meaning: because of the empty nature of the causes of suffering, the Bodhisattvas meditate on *kū* by means of the *Prajna paramita*, and in doing so their heart is free of all attachment and therefore free of all fear; they do not twist their mind up with thinking or imagining, and they enter the ultimate realm.

> By means of the *Prajna paramita*, all Buddhas of the Three Worlds – past, present and future – can attain ultimate, perfect enlightenment.

This statement that all the Buddhas of the past, present and future are able to attain the great enlightenment is also saying that all humans can do likewise.

> Therefore know that the *Prajna paramita* is a mantra of great and extraordinary power, a marvellous mantra, the ultimate mantra unequalled by all others. It removes all suffering, and is true, without falsity.

A mantra (*shingon*) is literally 'true words', the words of the Buddha. Because of its power, the words are often chanted like a spell.

> Therefore speak these words of the *Prajna paramita* – *gaté gaté paragaté parasamgaté bodhi svaha!*

The Relationship between the Three Sets of the Eighteen Realms

The Eighteen Realms		
The Six Consciousnesses. Mental products of reactions between the Sense Organs and Sense Objects	The Twelve Senses	
	The Six Sense Objects. External objects perceived by the Six Sense Organs	The Six Sense Organs. The physical sense organs

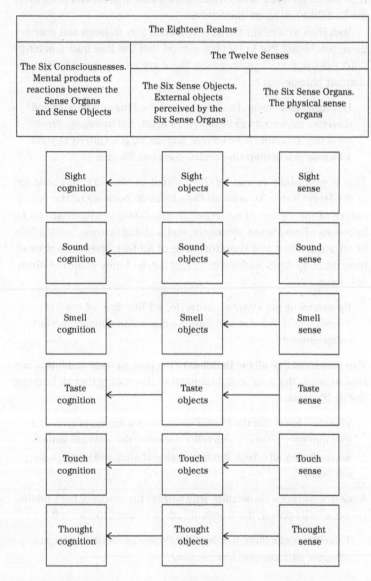

Sight cognition	Sight objects	Sight sense
Sound cognition	Sound objects	Sound sense
Smell cognition	Smell objects	Smell sense
Taste cognition	Taste objects	Taste sense
Touch cognition	Touch objects	Touch sense
Thought cognition	Thought objects	Thought sense

The words of the mantra, which are spoken directly in Sanskrit, are shrouded in mystery, but a possible translation might be: 'You who go, you who go, you who go to the Other Shore, oh enlightenment, oh joy.'

Some say that to chant this mantra is the final message of the Heart Sutra, but to me it seems more like a joyous exclamation, something like crying 'Oh how wonderful!' when you witness marvellous fireworks. Maybe that's not a very good analogy. Think of it as a kind of blessing or benediction on the power of this sutra.

When You See the World through the Eyes of Kū

We've now come to the end of a read-through of the Heart Sutra, though of course there is still much that I haven't explained completely. Let me finally just sum up in my own words.

In our everyday life, when we see something we might say, 'Ah, that's an X', stating its accepted name.

As we do this, we're also simultaneously calling to mind our pre-conceived idea or concept about this X. We're also applying instant judgements – it's a good thing or a bad thing, useful or not useful, beautiful or ugly, etc. And if we've had previous experience of this kind of thing called X we apply those memories – for instance memories of drinking water, or whatever it might be – so they also come into our mind and add judgements and feelings to our response to this X.

But this is the cause of suffering.

This world we believe we're living in here and now is essentially a world perceived through human eyes. Once we realize this and see the world through the eyes of *kū*, although sickness, old age and death exist as facts, the suffering that comes from them disappears. They are simply phenomena. It's just that by looking at them through our human eyes, we impose our negative judgements and feelings on them. The Heart Sutra teaches that we should throw away these prejudiced ways of seeing things, we should see and acknowledge a thing simply as that thing. This teaching is related to the story I told in Chapter 1 about the mosquitoes, where I had to learn not to see and experience them in a way that put myself, the human viewpoint, at the centre.

You can understand this with your mind, but it's not so easy to actually put it into practice. You can tell yourself that sickness, old age and death are just what they are, there's nothing intrinsically bad about them, but it's not so easy to really convince yourself of that, is it?

I think it's good enough just to know that there is this way of looking at things. I believe that there's real value in simply pausing in the midst of the various situations of life and saying to yourself, 'How would this look when seen with the eyes of *kū*?'

Zen practice is in a sense a way of cultivating the eyes of *kū*. Zen monks devote themselves to meditation in order to understand *kū* not just with the mind, but to become one with it through and through.

A *Kū* Tea Ceremony

The Buddha's Tea Bowl

One day at the beginning of spring, near the end of February when the air was still chilly, our teacher Sōen suddenly announced, 'We're having a *kū* tea ceremony.'

He marched briskly out of the main hall, hastily followed by myself and two others, Mr T and Mr K, who were there from Tokyo. My role at the time was teacher's attendant, accompanying him all day and looking after his various needs.

What on earth could he be up to now? I wondered, bewildered.

We followed him out and he led us to the plum orchard, less than five minutes from the main hall. There were about sixty plum trees there, smothered in splendid blossom. The plum orchard was a long, rather narrow north–south rectangular patch of land on a gentle west-facing slope.

'Right, this will do. Here's a good place.'

The place he'd chosen was a special place to sit deep among the plum blossoms, looking out to Hakone Mountain to the north and Tenjō Mountain to the south.

We sat down around him. It was beautiful with the petals drifting down around us, wafted on an occasional breeze.

Sōen abruptly turned to Mr T and said, 'What tea bowl would you like?'

Of course there wasn't a tea bowl in sight.

Mr T and Mr K were close followers of Sōen and visited the temple several times a year. Seeing no such thing as a tea bowl in front of them, they couldn't think what to answer.

After a pause Mr T said with a slightly puzzled air, 'I'll leave it up to you, Master.'

No tea bowl, no tea, no tea cakes . . . This was supposed to be a tea ceremony, but where was the kettle? Where was the hot water? Sōen took no notice of the three of us beside him who sat there looking stunned, he just grinned happily to himself.

'OK, you have Zen Master Rinzai's bowl, Mr T, and Mr K, you can have Zen Master Eisai's bowl.'

He set about going through the motions of putting powdered tea in a bowl, pouring in hot water and whisking it up to make a bowl of tea.

'Ryū-san, you have Zen Master Hakuin's bowl,' he said to me.

Then he took up the three bowls in turn, cupping each in his two hands, and handed them one by one to each of us.

'Ah, this is the one I'll have. The Buddha's bowl.' With this, he carefully set about making a fourth bowl of tea.

Unsure how to drink this non-existent tea, we followed his actions as he drank down his own.

'Oooh, that was delicious!' he declared loudly, and we all burst out laughing.

We sat there chatting for a while, then I remembered that we hadn't yet offered any actual tea to our guests.

'Master, I'd like to make tea back in the building now,' I said.

'Tea?'

'Yes.'

'But we've finished tea.'

'But that tea was non-existent.'

'Not non-existent. *Kū*.'

'?'

'You can't drink non-existent tea, but you *can* drink *kū* tea.'

'??'

'You see,' he continued, 'the actual bowl that the Buddha drank from isn't here, but we can drink bowl after bowl of the tea of "*kū*" that he preached.'

We were even more puzzled.

After that, Sōen held quite a few more '*kū* tea ceremonies'. There's simply no knowing what Zen monks will get up to!

Look at the Caterpillar

Another time, as we were going through the plum orchard, Sōen said to me, 'Well now, Ryū-san. You stay here for a while and look at the plum blossom.'

'Uh-oh, here we go again,' I almost said aloud. But when I turned around he'd already gone, leaving me there alone while he walked back towards the main hall. There was nothing for it but to stay there and watch the blossoms.

So there I stood, looking at the plum blossoms.

Well, I thought, they're pretty things so that's OK.

Come to think of it, why do they flower, I wonder?

Do they just flower, without thought or plan?

I stood there looking at the plum blossoms with these foolish thoughts going through my mind until after a while I got tired of them, and lay down in a patch of sunlight.

How long did I lie there peacefully? Suddenly I heard Sōen's distant voice – 'Hey, Ryū-san!'

'Y-yes!' I called back, flustered. I'd slipped into that delicious world of sleep where you enter a selflessness that transcends time and space.

Then on another day he said to me again, 'Stay here and watch for a while.' This time he was pointing to a caterpillar that was wriggling along a fallen branch on the ground.

'Watch until you see this caterpillar shining with light.'

With that, Sōen put his palms together reverently in front of the caterpillar, then away he went.

So there I stayed, doing as I was told and watching the caterpillar. I'd never watched a caterpillar this close up before. But watching so intently, I found the way it wriggled along the branch a bit creepy.

'Yuk, it's pretty disgusting,' I said to myself.

Why had Sōen made that gesture of reverence to it? Was it because all living things are sacred?

After a while I simply couldn't keep gazing at the caterpillar any longer, so I left.

There were other similar occasions.

'Let's watch Venus until it disappears.'

'Let's just look at Mount Fuji over there.'

'Let's look at a glass of water.'

Sōen would never comment on these things, but I think this was his own special way of giving a teaching.

The $k\bar{u}$ tea ceremony was really about contemplating the realm of the Buddha's enlightenment. He was comparing the realm of enlightenment to a $k\bar{u}$ tea ceremony.

The same goes for watching Venus. The star's light is the realm of enlightenment, the realm of $k\bar{u}$. That light utterly illuminates us.

As for watching the plum blossoms or the caterpillar, they lead to the question, 'So what were you thinking as you watched? Perhaps you thought, "What pretty blossoms", or "What a horrible caterpillar"? But that's just your thoughts, it wasn't that pretty blossoms or a horrible caterpillar were actually there. Enough of this "I'm looking" or "I think". Look with the eyes of $k\bar{u}$.'

That's surely what he really intended to tell me.

Trees and plants, flowers and caterpillars, stars and all the other things in the natural world can't speak, but we can hear the Buddha's teachings through this world. This is called 'teaching the Law through unfeeling things'. From time to time, Sōen would teach us the Heart Sutra in this way.

In other words, his plan was that we should perceive the realm of *kū* by really looking at things – change looking into true perception.

You look at plum blossoms, or a caterpillar, or Mount Fuji, and you have various ideas and feelings about them. Then you do away with these ideas and feelings, and what opens up for you instead is the realm of true perception.

For this to happen, what you need to do is to take your time and look deeply.

Think again of those opening words of the Heart Sutra: 'Through the deep practice of *Prajna paramita*, Kannon Bodhisattva perceived that all the Five Aggregates were *kū*, and was liberated from all suffering.' In all things, deep or dedicated practice is essential. It seems I

I wonder why plum blossoms are called plum blossoms?

Head slowly leaning further and further sideways as time passes and the earth turns.

still didn't really do this, whether it was in looking at plum blossoms, looking at a caterpillar or looking at Mount Fuji.

I still think of how Sōen told me to look at Venus – that same Morning Star that shone when the Buddha's mind filled with the light of enlightenment – and watch until it disappeared. His words are with me as I look at it today.

Afterword

It's almost time to leave you.

I've tried to give you an idea of what Zen practice is by talking about *kōans*, meditation, monastic begging, the practice of physical work in the monastery, food, and then by giving a quick introduction to the history of Zen and to the Heart Sutra's realm of *kū*.

Finally, I'd like to tell you my ideas about just what meaning and effect this practice has, and how it relates to normal, everyday life.

The Effects of Zen Meditation

Imagine there's a cup of dirty water in front of you, with mud and water all mixed up together.

Now let's take the time to wait and watch and see what happens.

Slowly but surely it starts to separate out. The mud sinks until it's all lying at the bottom, while the water above it is now pure and translucent.

This is what happens with Zen meditation, it seems to me.

The mud is our worldly desires. When these desires are swirling around in us – in other words when the water is all mixed up with swirling mud – we are suffering.

'I love her so, why can't she understand how I feel?'

'I hope I never see his face again!'

'I swear I'm going to make it in the world!'

'I want to be rich!'

'I wish I could be slim!'

Our minds are tortured by so many different kinds of desire,

101

depending on who we are. Popular Buddhism sums these up as 'the 108 Desires'. But stop and think a moment and you'll realize that wanting this or that, or hating something else, doesn't help you achieve what you long for. Things usually don't work out that way. And desires are difficult things – if you leave them alone they can grow and swell till they're quite out of control. It happens a lot, doesn't it?

Now take up the meditation position, control your mind, your body and your breath. Remember, there's no such thing as someone without desires, so just let them be, don't be attached, stay sitting with your mind like clear water, and maintain that state.

If you were in a monastery you wouldn't just do this once a day, it would be many times a day, in fact all day long. You can see why it's a perfect environment for maintaining the clarity of that water.

The same thing goes for begging for alms or for physical work. As I said in Chapter 2, meditation involves controlling mind, body and breath, while begging and physical work involve controlling the body in motion.

But this still leaves a question. The water in the top of the glass looks clear and translucent, but how clear is it, really? You won't know unless you do a quality test.

The teacher is the one to test its quality and apply the necessary guidance. While you're practising Zen in a monastery, every day there is a question-and-answer session between the teacher and the monk. This is how the teacher finds out how clear the water in each glass really is. And *kōans* are the standard he can use to make this judgement.

This translucent water can be put into action in various ways. You can use it to enjoy drinking tea, or when you cook. You can use it to wash dirty things, or to blend various things together. It can be freely used in all sorts of different ways, depending on the situation.

This is the use of Zen practice in normal everyday life. Our day-to-day life is the place where the pure water is put into practice. There's no point in just sitting and looking at the pure water we've managed to achieve. Its true meaning lies in applying it in everyday life. At the same time, everyday life also has the function of further purifying the water.

It seems like a contradiction, but the fact is that the place of Zen practice is not just the meditation hall. Getting up in the morning, folding your bedding and washing your face is also Zen practice. So is cooking food, so is eating it. When you fold your bedding, that's all you're doing. When you wash your face, that's all you're doing. When you cook you just cook, you concentrate solely on that, you don't think of anything else, your whole self is focused there – this is the true essence of Zen. There is no end to one's practice. Putting that pure water freely into practice in your everyday life, you not only maintain its purity but continue to purify it. In other words, your whole life until the day you die is Zen practice.

It's Because You are a Buddha That You Can Do Zen Practice

So if you pursue this practice, will you eventually arrive at buddhahood? No. That's not the way Zen thinks.

The great Zen master Hakuin said, 'Our original nature is buddhahood. Be enlightened to your own nature and you will know that this physical self is none other than buddha.'

These words are said to express the essence of Rinzai Zen teaching. They could be re-stated like this: 'We are all fundamentally buddhas. If we perceive our own buddha nature, we and the Buddha are one.'

Through our practice, we perceive our own buddha nature. Therefore, Hakuin's words could be summed up as meaning 'a buddha becomes a buddha through his or her practice'. This is very important for an understanding of Zen – it's not that normal people become buddhas through their practice, but that buddhas do. In other words, it's because we are essentially buddhas that we can pursue our practice.

To express this in terms of the metaphor of the glass of water, we all have deep within us the beautiful pure water of our buddha nature. Once we perceive the existence of this water and leave the mud of our desires, we open up a world where this boundless pure water can be applied everywhere.

Anyway, this is how it seems to me.

AFTERWORD

Looking back on my time spent in the monastery, I'm aware of my great good fortune in being taught simultaneously by not one but two wonderful teachers, and I thank my karma that I had the opportunity to meet them.

The things I learned from them only grow deeper with the passing years. It has often happened since I left the monastery and became a temple priest that I've suddenly understood what something back then was really about. It's just a huge shame that I can no longer ask them about it in person, but I believe that within their words and teachings lies a boundless world that transcends time and space.

The Heart Sutra
(as it is chanted in Japan)

Maka hannya haramita shingyō

*The Central Sutra of the Great
Wisdom of Enlightenment*

*Kanjizai bosa gyōjin hannya haramita ji shōken goun kaikū
doissai kuyaku.*
Through the deep practice of *Prajna paramita*, Kannon Bodhisattva perceived that all the Five Aggregates were *kū*, and was
liberated from all suffering.

*Shari shi shiki fu i kū kū fu i shiki shiki soku ze kū kū soku ze
shiki ju sō gyō shiki yaku bu nyo ze*
Oh Sariputra, form is not other than *kū*, *kū* is not other than form.
Form is *kū*, *kū* is form. This is also true of sensation, perception,
volition and consciousness.

Shari shi ze sho hō kū sō fu shō fu metsu fu ku fu jō fu zō fu gen
Sariputra, all dharmas are in their nature emptiness, neither born
nor extinguished, neither foul nor pure, neither increasing nor
decreasing.

*Ze ko kū chū mu shiki mu ju sō gyō shiki mu gen ni bi zesshin
ni mu shiki shō kō mi soku hō mu gen kai nai shi mu i shiki kai*

105

For this reason, in *kū* there are no form, no sensation, perception, volition, consciousness. No eyes, ears, nose, tongue, body or mind. No sight, sound, scent, taste, touch or phenomena. No world of seeing, through to no world of consciousness.

Mu mu myō yaku mu mu myō jin nai shi mu rō shi yaku mu rō shi jin mu ku shū metsu dō mu chi yaku mu toku
No ignorance, also no extinction of ignorance; no ageing, no death, also no extinction of ageing and death. No suffering, no cause of suffering, no cessation, no path; no wisdom, no attainment.

I mu sho totsu ko bo dai satta e han nya ha ra mi ta ko shin mu ke ge mu ke ge ko mu u ku fu on ri issai ten dō mu sō ku gyō ne han
Having no attainment, Bodhisattvas rely on *Prajna paramita* and therefore have no attachment in their heart, and having no attachment they therefore have no fear, and having gone utterly beyond all wrong perceptions they realize complete Nirvana.

San ze sho butsu e han nya ha ra mi ta ko toku a noku ta ra san myaku san bo dai
By means of the *Prajna paramita*, all Buddhas of the Three Worlds – past, present and future – can attain ultimate, perfect enlightenment.

Ko chi han nya ha ra mi ta ze dai jin shu ze dai myō shu ze mu jō shu ze mu tō dō shu nō jo issai ku shin jitsu fu ko
Therefore know that the *Prajna paramita* is a mantra of great and extraordinary power, a marvellous mantra, the ultimate mantra unequalled by all others. It removes all suffering, and is true, without falsity.

Ko setsu han nya ha ra mi ta shu soku setsu shu watsu gya tei gya tei ha ra gya tei hara sō gya tei bō ji sowa ka han nya shin gyō

Therefore speak this mantra of the *Prajna paramita – gaté gaté paragaté parasamgaté bodhi svaha*!

Many other translations of the Heart Sutra exist. You could also try the following:

Kazuaki Tanahashi, *The Heart Sutra: A Comprehensive Guide to the Classic of Mahayana Buddhism* (Shambhala Publications, 2015)

Red Pine, *The Heart Sutra: Translation and Commentary* (Counterpoint Press, 2005)

Thich Nhat Han, *The Other Shore: A New Translation of the Heart Sutra with Commentaries* (Palm Leaves Press, 2017)

Glossary

BODHISATTVA: An enlightened being committed to the salvation of others.

DENSU: The monk responsible for leading sutra chanting and rituals.

DŌJŌ: Place where training for meditation or martial arts takes place, including place of training for monks (monastery).

ENPATSU: Begging in a place some distance from the monastery.

FUSÉ: The gifts offered to monks and priests by lay people; generous giving.

FŪSU: Monastery book-keeper.

FUZUI: The monk in charge of financial and miscellaneous matters in the monastery.

GASSHŌ: A gesture of reverence, with the hands held in front of the chest, palms pressed together.

HANKA FUZA: Half-lotus meditation position.

HONDŌ: Main hall, where sutras are chanted and ceremonies are conducted.

HONZAN: Main temple to which lesser temples are affiliated.

HŌ: 'The Law'. The Japanese term for the Buddhist doctrine.

INJI: A *rōshi*'s personal attendant.

JIHATSU: Nest of bowls belonging to a monk, used for meals.

JIKIJITSU: The position immediately below *rōshi*.

JISHIKI: *Zendō* attendant.

JOKEI: Junior officer under the *jikijitsu*.

109

KANBAN-BUKURO: Bag used for begging.

KANNAZEN: Zen that makes use of *kōan* study.

KANNON: The Bodhisattva of Compassion, often depicted as female. Known as Kuan Yin in Chinese and Avalokitesvara in Sanskrit.

KEISAKU: A long thin stick, wielded to help monks concentrate in their meditation.

KEKKA FUZA: Full-lotus meditation position.

KESA: Monk's robe.

KŌAN: A story containing a seemingly insoluble puzzle that the Zen practitioner meditates on until the answer is intuitively rather than rationally understood. An important meditation tool in the Rinzai Zen tradition.

KŪ: Literally 'emptiness' or 'void'. A key concept in Zen Buddhism.

KYŌDŌ: Sutra hall, housing a collection of sutras.

MONDŌ: Literally 'question-and-answer'. The discussion of religious questions that takes place in the interview between teacher and student.

MU: Literally 'nothing' or 'not'. A key concept in Zen Buddhism.

MUMONKAN: Literally 'The Gateless Barrier'. A collection of forty-eight *kōans* written in Sung dynasty China by a monk called Mumon Ekai (1183–1260).

PRAJNA PARAMITA *(HANNYA HARAMITA* IN JAPANESE*)*: Sanskrit term meaning the perfect wisdom of enlightenment, profound insight. The name of the Heart Sutra.

RINZAI: One of the two main schools of Zen Buddhism.

RŌSHI: Zen teacher.

SAMU: Manual labour in the monastery.

SANMON: Temple gate.

SANZEN: Private meeting between teacher and student for purposes of instruction.

SANZEN NO MA: Room where the *sanzen* meeting takes place.

SAREI: Formal or less formal serving of tea in the monastery.

SESSHIN: Intensive meditation session lasting a number of days.

SHIKA: The monk in charge of the administration of the monastery overall.

SHINTŌ: Monks in their first year at the monastery.

SHŌJIN RYŌRI: Zen vegetarian food.

SŌSAN: Formal session in which all the monks meet the *rōshi* one by one in order of rank.

SŌTŌ: One of the two main schools of Zen Buddhism.

SUTRA: Sacred Buddhist scripture.

TAKUHATSU: Begging rounds performed by monks, usually in the vicinity of the temple.

TENZO: Monastery kitchen. Also the name of the head cook.

UNSUI: 'Cloud and water'. A Zen monk in training.

ZAFU: Meditation cushion.

ZAZEN: Zen meditation.

ZENDŌ: Meditation hall, where monks live and meditate.